CORNELSEN
SENIOR
ENGLISH
LIBRARY

WILLIAM SHAKESPEARE

Hamlet

Cornelsen

William Shakespeare **Hamlet**

Textbearbeitung, Annotationen und Zusatzmaterialien: Peter und Martina Baasner
Verlagsredaktion: Dr. Georg-Christian v. Raumer
Lizenzmanagement: Britta Bensmann
Umschlaggestaltung: Cornelsen Verlag Design/Klein & Halm Grafikdesign
Umschlagillustration: stock.adobe.com/Danilkin Gennady/Diflope
Layout und technische Umsetzung: L101 Mediengestaltung, Fürstenwalde

Picture acknowledgements: p. 299: Bridgeman Images/© Look and Learn English
School (19th century), p. 301: Bridgeman Images/Peter Phipp/Travelshots

www.cornelsen.de

1. Auflage, 2. Druck 2022

Alle Drucke dieser Auflage sind inhaltlich unverändert und
können im Unterricht nebeneinander verwendet werden.

Druck: H. Heenemann, Berlin

ISBN 978-3-06-036024-6

Contents

Introduction

Since it was first performed at the Globe Theatre in London in 1601, hardly any other play has received the same amount of attention as *Hamlet*. It is a classic of world literature and probably the most famous play in the world. Numerous publications have been written about *Hamlet* and detailed historical, cultural and literary research has been done to explain its meaning as well as the hero's character and motivation. It is also the longest play Shakespeare wrote, with Hamlet on stage two thirds of the time and speaking more than 1500 lines. The full text version of about 4000 words will last four hours, which is why directors usually cut the text to some extent. Since no manuscripts of Shakespeare's plays have survived, editors make use of either the two earliest printed versions with differing additions or cuts (*Quarto 1*, 1603, and *Quarto 2*, 1604) and/or the compilation of his plays put together by fellow actors after his death, the *First Folio* (1623).

Like the other dramatists of his time, Shakespeare used the plots of plays, stories and poems he may have studied in school or seen on stage. The story of Hamlet (called Amleth) was as part of Danish folklore and was first written down by Saxo Grammaticus in the 12th century (published in the *Historiae Danicae* in 1514). A French version appeared in François de Belleforest's *Histoires Tragiques* (1514), whose English translation (1608) was probably available to Shakespeare. Another version, the '*Ur-Hamlet*', usually attributed to Elizabethan dramatist Thomas Kyd, seems to have existed at the time, but was lost. Shakespeare took elements from these versions, but reworked the material to a great extent. His singular gift of coining new words, using imagery and rhetorical devices to create memorable lines explains the fact that a great number of quotes from his plays are still used in modern speech. Even people who do not know the play will have heard 'To be or not to be, that is the question' in another context, and phrases like 'There is something rotten in the state of Denmark', 'Brevity is the soul of wit' or 'The rest is silence' are commonly quoted.

Hamlet is also one of the most frequently performed plays in the world, popular among audiences and actors alike. The title role is seen as the crowning achievement of a male or female actor's career, and the reception of a new performance concentrates on the latest famous actor who played him. Hamlet is an actor himself in a way and has strong ideas about acting, which might make the part doubly attractive. The role offers much diverse dramatic action and intense conflict in human relationships and familial contexts many viewers can relate to.

Hamlet invites the audience to share his innermost feelings as well as the working of his mind. Often, he is the only focus for the audience's attention, to whom he speaks directly in long soliloquies. Despite his introspection, he is a character given to impulsive actions and is exciting to watch, which might explain the continuing fascination with this complex and enigmatic character.

In the 19th century, he was interpreted as a sensitive, romantic hero incapable of rash action, and later as an intellectual who cannot transform his complex emotions into action. In some modern concepts, he is seen as an individual struggling against injustice, supervision and political oppression – there have been innumerable interpretations by actors, directors and critics.

In modern culture, the image of Hamlet, who seems to exist apart from his play, has become an easily recognized icon – a man in black holding up a skull. The writer and critic T.S. Eliot called him 'The Mona Lisa of literature' (*The Sacred Wood*, 1922).

In terms of spinoffs, Hamlet's afterlife is impressive too. A wealth of adaptations in different genres and rewritings of the plot have been created for over 400 years, and the play still resonates today. It was and is read in various ways, e.g. as

- a story of revenge, which was a very popular type of tragedy at Shakespeare's time. Although Hamlet is unusual in questioning his mission, the idea to exact retribution on those who have wronged you appealed to viewers, even if vengeance was forbidden by law and the church. *Hamlet* is not a straightforward revenge drama, although it contains many of the typical elements of classical revenge tragedy, e.g. a melancholy avenger, a villain obsessed by passions, ghosts, madness and even a play within the play;

- a political struggle for the Danish throne in which King Claudius has assassinated his brother, Old Hamlet, to seize the crown and stolen the succession that rightfully belongs to Young Hamlet; the prince, who in turn carries out a personal vendetta against his uncle to regain the throne;
- a study in grief, in which three sons lose their fathers killed violently in their absence and seek revenge, either by assignment or of their own volition;
- an analysis of depression, in which Hamlet is unable to deal with the blows of fate he encounters, suffers from indecision or procrastination and reflects suicide;
- a Freudian interpretation of Hamlet unconsciously feeling hatred for his mother's new husband and sorrow for her hasty remarriage, more than for his father's death, which reflects the concept of the Oedipus guilt complex;
- a play about the demands made by fathers manipulating their adult children and its appropriateness in regard to the fatal consequences the younger generation have to suffer;
- a coming-of-age story with a misunderstood hero thrust into a broken world he is unprepared to fix and trying to make sense of. Alone, friendless and betrayed by most people around him, having lost a father, his girlfriend and the trust in his mother, Hamlet tries to take on responsibility in an extremely complicated situation. He blames his elders for their inconstancy and moral shortcomings and has no outlet for his pent-up feelings.

Apart from these many different possible views, this play of ideas also offers a multitude of questions that have been discussed since its first performance and cannot be interpreted in just one way, e.g. whether Hamlet truly loved Ophelia as he claims in Act V or whether Gertrude was aware of the murder plots her new husband hatched. Many open questions remain, and here, one of Hamlet's famous quotes can be applied perfectly: 'There is nothing either good or bad, but thinking makes it so.' (II, ii, 242–243)

The Language of Shakespeare

Shakespeare's language is not easy to understand, not even for a modern-day native speaker of English. Since Shakespeare's time, the English language has changed quite considerably. As a result, many words are no longer in use or have a different meaning. Through it all, Shakespeare remains a great influence today and his words still echo down the centuries, as generations have read and enjoyed his plays. With a little bit of effort, his language can still be appreciated today. Although annotations on the left-hand pages will offer you more than adequate help when reading the play, it would be useful to be aware of some general points before you start reading. Here are a few tips on how to deal with Shakespeare's language.

Vocabulary

While Shakespeare used many words that are no longer in use in modern English, e.g. 'climatures' (= territories), I, i, 125 or 'romage' (= hectic activity), I, i, 107, many of the words he used have changed their meaning:

Such was the very armour he had on. (I, i, 60)

'Very' meant 'genuine, real, true' besides having the meaning it has today.
'Hap(pi)ly' meant 'perhaps' (III, i, 167) and 'still' was used for 'always' (I, v, 188).

Sentence structure

Shakespeare's structure differs from modern English syntax. The positioning of parts of the sentence depended on the emphasis they were given and on the rhythm of the line. Shakespeare wrote mostly in blank verse, i.e. regular metrical but unrhymed lines. Usually this was iambic pentameter, a rhythm with five stressed syllables to a line along the following pattern: di-dum, di-dum, di-dum, di-dum, di-dum, with the stress being on 'dum'.

Come, go with me. I will go seek the king. (II, i, 100)

Sometimes Shakespeare deviates from this rule when a line needs eleven syllables or exclamations are used.

Revenge his foul and most unnatural murder. (I, v, 25)

When the characters' emotions run high, this is mirrored in the irregular metre of their speech.

How now? A rat! Dead for a ducat, dead! (III, iv, 25)

Say, why is this? Wherefore? What should we do? (I, iv, 57)

Shakespeare also frequently splits a line between two characters to keep the pattern.

POLONIUS: Mad for thy love?
OPHELIA: My lord, I do not know.
                                                        (II, i, 84)

Shakespeare altered his prose – and often the intonation or pronunciation of words (indicated here by an accent, e.g. 'ĕ') – to make it more suitable to verse. It is worth collecting the words of a sentence and rearranging them in a logical way to understand what the sentence means. Always look for the main verb and the subject first. Here are examples of sentences with an unusual structure:

Cannot you tell that? (V, i, 132)

Man delights not me. (II, ii, 295)

As Shakespeare liked using clauses, his sentences often seem long and complicated. That is why it is important to find first the main verb and the subject. Shakespeare also made frequent use of enjambement, or run-on lines, which have no pause at the end of the line but flow into the next one(s). When you read the verses aloud, you should breathe in when punctuation marks are used in order to be able to get through the passage fluently. See, for instance, Claudius's speech in I, ii, 1–16 and Horatio's in I, i, 79–95.

Note that many of Shakespeare's relative clauses would be separate sentences in modern English. 'Which' etc. is often used to link what could be another sentence onto a previous sentence. See Claudius in III, i, 163 ('which for to prevent …') for an example.

Rhyme

Most of Shakespeare's verse does not rhyme. Sometimes, however, he used rhyming couplets in order to make something more memorable or express the emotions a character experiences much better. Thus, Hamlet says:

> The time is out of joint: O cursèd spite,
> That ever I was born to set it right.
>
> (I, v, 191–192)

In songs sung by Hamlet (III, ii, 252–255, 261–264) or the First Clown (V, i, 57–60, 66–69, 86–89), Shakespeare uses an alternating meter of eight and six beats to suit the melody. To emphasize Ophelia's madness, her songs are set in a broken meter suggesting her confused state (IV, v, 23–26, 38–40, 48–55, 58–66, 164–166, 183, 186–195). Tetrameter (four beats to a line) and rhyme are used in the prologue to the play *The Murder of Gonzago* (III, ii, 133–135), and the decisive moment (when the play's murderer uses poison) is marked by three rhyming couplets of eleven and ten beats (III, ii, 236–241).

Imagery

Shakespeare often uses imagery – words that stand for more than their basic or literal meaning and thus become images in the mind – in order to help the reader understand a character's thoughts and emotions.

> When sorrows come, they come not single spies,
> But in battalions.
>
> (IV, v, 76–77)

Auxiliary 'do'

In Shakespeare's time, the auxiliary 'do' in interrogative and negative forms was not always used.

What means this, my lord? (III, ii, 124)

I loved you not. (III, i, 117)

On the other hand, the auxiliary 'do' without any special emphasis can be found in positive statements.

And I do doubt the hatch and the disclose
Will be some danger.

(III, i, 162–163)

Auxiliary 'be'

'Be' as an auxiliary was used to form compound tenses of certain intransitive verbs in Elizabethan English, especially 'come' and 'go' (as is the case in German).

Where is he gone? (IV, i, 23) – Where has he gone?

Second-person pronouns

In 16th-century English there were two forms of 'you':

– 'thou' (object form: 'thee', possessive determiner: 'thy', 'thine'). In Shakespeare's time, servants and children were addressed as 'thou' (in the singular). Moreover, the common people (and intimate friends) used this form of address with each other.

Get thee to a nunnery! Why wouldst thou be a breeder of sinners? (III, i, 119–120)
– 'ye/you' (object form: 'you', possessive determiner: 'your'). In Shakespeare's time 'ye/you' was used as a term of respect for individuals ('Sie') or as the second-person plural form ('ihr').

Why did you laugh then, when I said 'Man delights not me'?
(II, ii, 299–300)

Possessive determiners

In Elizabethan English, 'mine' and 'thine' as possessive determiners were sometimes used instead of 'my' and 'thy' when placed before vowels and before 'h'. 'Thine' and 'mine' were also used in much the same way as 'mine' is today (as possessive determiners).

And let thine eye look like a friend on Denmark. (I, ii, 69)

Verb endings

– The third-person singular verb endings: In Shakespeare's time, the third-person singular verb often ended in '-th', e.g. 'doth' (does), 'hath' (has).

singeth (I, i, 160)

turneth (IV, vii, 20)

– The second-person singular verb endings: In Shakespeare's time, the second-person verb after 'thou' ended in '-st', e.g. 'canst', 'dost', 'didst', 'sayest', 'hast', 'art' (verb: be), or, in the case of 'will' and 'shall', 'wilt' and 'shalt'.

Ha, ha, boy, sayest thou so? (I, v, 150)

What wilt thou do for her? (V, i, 252)

What have I done, that thou dar'st wag thy tongue.
In noise so rude against me? (III, iv, 40–41)

Hold off thy hand! (V, i, 244)

– The past participle of some verbs was shortened.

hath oped (I, iv, 50) – opened

Would/will

'Would' often means 'want' or 'wish'.

> I would you did, sir. (V, ii, 126) – I wish you did, sir.

Subjunctive

In Elizabethan English the subjunctive was still widely used.

> O, there be players that I have seen play. (III, ii, 24–25) – There are players that I have seen play.

Compounds

Shakespeare often used compounds to express an idea for which modern English needs a phrase.

> this something-settled matter in his heart (III, i, 169) – this partly-fixed matter

But

'But' has a variety of meanings, e.g. 'only', 'just', 'without it being the case that …' and 'except'. For examples, see I, ii, 86 und 138.

Adverbs

For a German speaker, some Elizabethan adverbs of place and relative adverbs are easier to understand than for a modern English speaker.

thence (*dahin*)	wherein (*worin*)
whence (*woher*)	wherewith (*womit*)
hence (*hierher*)	wherefore (*wofür, weshalb, warum*)

Omission of consonant

In order to reflect everyday speech or cut a syllable to fit the metre, Shakespeare would leave out consonants (especially the 'v') in particular words.

e'er (ever)	an' (and)	ta'en (taken)
ne'er (never)	o' (on/of)	for't (for it)
o'er (over)	e'en (even)	'tis (it is)

The Characters

The Royal Family of Denmark

HAMLET	Prince of Denmark
CLAUDIUS	King of Denmark, Hamlet's uncle
GERTRUDE	Queen of Denmark, Hamlet's mother
GHOST	of King Hamlet, Hamlet's father

The court of Denmark

POLONIUS	Lord Chamberlain and counsellor to the king
OPHELIA	his daughter
LAERTES	his son
REYNALDO	his servant
OSRIC	a courtier
CORNELIUS **VOLTEMAND**	Danish ambassadors to Norway
MARCELLUS **BARNARDO** **FRANCISCO**	Officers of the Watch
HORATIO	friend to Prince Hamlet
ROSENCRANTZ **GUILDENSTERN**	former schoolfriends of Prince Hamlet
A LORD	
A GENTLEMAN	

A PRIEST

Norwegians

FORTINBRAS	Prince of Norway
CAPTAIN	in Fortinbras's army

Elsinore citizens and visitors

FIRST PLAYER
SECOND PLAYER
THIRD PLAYER   actors visiting Elsinore
FOURTH PLAYER

FIRST CLOWN	gravedigger
SECOND CLOWN	his assistant

ENGLISH AMBASSADORS

Sailors, citizens, lords and gentlemen, messengers and attendants, soldiers and guards

The action is set in and around the royal palace at Elsinore,
Denmark.

Summary:

On the gun platform of the royal Danish castle at Elsinore, the change of guards takes place at midnight. The soldiers feel unease because Norwegian forces led by Fortinbras are advancing and a ghost has been seen twice on the battlements. Prince Hamlet's friend Horatio has agreed to watch with the men and confirms their impression that the apparition looks like Denmark's dead king, Old Hamlet, in battle armour. Since it does not speak to them, Horatio decides to inform Hamlet of this occurrence.

Annotations:

- **2**   *nay:* no
       me: i.e. Francisco should have challenged Barnardo
       unfold: identify
- **6**   *carefully upon your hour:* punctually
- **8**   *relief:* release from sentry duty
- **9**   *sick at heart:* sad, melancholy
- **13**   *rivals:* partners
- **15**   *ground:* country
       liegemen to the Dane ['liːʤmen]: loyal followers of the Danish king
- **16**   *give:* God give

ACT I

Scene I

Elsinore. A platform before the castle.

Enter two guards; first, FRANCISCO, *who paces up and down at his post; then* BARNARDO, *who approaches him.*

BARNARDO: Who's there?
FRANCISCO: Nay, answer me. Stand and unfold yourself.
BARNARDO: Long live the king!
FRANCISCO: Barnardo?
5 **BARNARDO:** He.
FRANCISCO: You come most carefully upon your hour.
BARNARDO: 'Tis now struck twelve. Get thee to bed, Francisco.
FRANCISCO: For this relief much thanks. 'Tis bitter cold,
  And I am sick at heart.
10 **BARNARDO:** Have you had quiet guard?
FRANCISCO: Not a mouse stirring.
BARNARDO: Well, good night.
  If you do meet Horatio and Marcellus,
  The rivals of my watch, bid them make haste.

Enter HORATIO *and* MARCELLUS.

FRANCISCO: I think I hear them. Stand, ho! Who is there?
15 **HORATIO:** Friends to this ground.
MARCELLUS: And liegemen to the Dane.
FRANCISCO: Give you good night.
MARCELLUS: O, farewell, honest soldier.
  Who hath relieved you?
FRANCISCO: Barnardo hath my place.
  Give you good night.

23   *fantasy:* imagination
24   *let belief take hold of him:* believe
25   *touching:* concerning
         dreaded ['dredɪd]: feared
26   *entreated him along:* asked him earnestly to come along
27   *watch:* keep guard through
28   *apparition:* ghost, spirit
29   *approve our eyes:* confirm what we saw
31   *assail your ears:* tell you loudly
32   *fortified against:* shut to
36   *yond ... pole:* the North star
37   *t'illume:* to lighten, to illuminate
42   *scholar:* learned man speaking Latin (ghosts were thought to speak Latin)
43   *mark:* observe closely

Exit.

MARCELLUS:	Holla, Barnardo!
BARNARDO:	Say –

What, is Horatio there?

HORATIO: A piece of him.

20 **BARNARDO:** Welcome, Horatio. Welcome, good Marcellus.

MARCELLUS: What, has this thing appeared again tonight?

BARNARDO: I have seen nothing.

MARCELLUS: Horatio says 'tis but our fantasy,

And will not let belief take hold of him

25   Touching this dreaded sight, twice seen of us.

Therefore I have entreated him along,

With us to watch the minutes of this night,

That, if again this apparition come,

He may approve our eyes and speak to it.

30 **HORATIO:** Tush, tush, 'twill not appear.

BARNARDO: Sit down awhile,

And let us once again assail your ears,

That are so fortified against our story,

What we two nights have seen.

HORATIO: Well, sit we down,

And let us hear Barnardo speak of this.

35 **BARNARDO:** Last night of all,

When yond same star that's westward from the pole

Had made his course t'illume that part of heaven

Where now it burns, Marcellus and myself,

The bell then beating one –

Enter GHOST.

40 **MARCELLUS:** Peace! Break thee off! Look where it comes again!

BARNARDO: In the same figure, like the King that's dead.

MARCELLUS: Thou art a scholar; speak to it, Horatio.

BARNARDO: Looks it not like the king? Mark it, Horatio.

44 *harrows:* tortures
45 *would be spoke to:* wishes to be spoken to
46 *that usurp'st* [juːˈzɜːpst]: who wrongfully seizes
48 *buried Denmark:* dead King Hamlet
49 *sometimes:* formerly
charge: command (v)
50 *stalk* (v): walk
57 *sensible and true avouch:* proof
60 *armour:* metal clothing to protect the body in battle
61 *th'ambitious Norway:* the Norwegian king determined to succeed
combated: fought
62 *parle:* discussion; negotiation
63 *smote:* hit, attacked
the sledded Polacks: the Polish army on sledges
65 *jump:* exactly
66 *martial stalk:* military step
67 *in what particular thought to work:* what to make of this
68 *gross and scope:* general view
69 *this ... state:* foreshadows disaster for Denmark
71 *strict and most observant:* dutiful
72 *toils the subject of the land:* wearies the citizens of the state

HORATIO: Most like. It harrows me with fear and wonder.

45 **BARNARDO:** It would be spoke to.

MARCELLUS: Question it, Horatio.

HORATIO: What art thou that usurp'st this time of night
    Together with that fair and warlike form
    In which the majesty of buried Denmark
    Did sometimes march? By heaven I charge thee speak!

50 **MARCELLUS:** It is offended.

BARNARDO: See, it stalks away!

HORATIO: Stay! Speak, speak! I charge thee speak!

Exit GHOST.

MARCELLUS: 'Tis gone and will not answer.

BARNARDO: How now, Horatio? You tremble and look pale.
    Is not this something more than fantasy?

55   What think you on't?

HORATIO: Before my God, I might not this believe
    Without the sensible and true avouch
    Of mine own eyes.

MARCELLUS: Is it not like the king?

HORATIO: As thou art to thyself.

60   Such was the very armour he had on
    When he th' ambitious Norway combated.
    So frowned he once when, in an angry parle,
    He smote the sledded Polacks on the ice.
    'Tis strange.

65 **MARCELLUS:** Thus twice before, and jump at this dead hour,
    With martial stalk hath he gone by our watch.

HORATIO: In what particular thought to work I know not;
    But, in the gross and scope of my opinion,
    This bodes some strange eruption to our state.

70 **MARCELLUS:** Good now, sit down, and tell me he that knows,
    Why this same strict and most observant watch
    So nightly toils the subject of the land,

73 *cast* (n): production of a metal object
        brazen: made of brass (*Messing*)
74 *foreign mart* (v): trade with foreign countries
        implement: equipment
75 *impress:* enforcement of labour, conscription
        shipwright: shipbuilder
77 *what ... toward:* what is going on
78 *joint-labourer:* fellow worker
80 *whisper:* rumour
83 *thereto pricked on:* urged to
        emulate: jealous
84 *dared:* challenged
        valiant: courageous
85 *esteem* (v): regard
86 *slay:* kill
        sealed compact: confirmed treaty
87 *ratified:* made valid
        law and heraldry: conventions of nobility
88 *forfeit* ['fɔ:fɪt]: lose
89 *stood seized of:* lost
        conqueror: winner
90 *a moiety competent:* an equal portion
91 *gagèd:* put a bet on
        had returned: would have gone
92 *inheritance:* possessions
93 *vanquisher:* winner
93–94 *as ... designed:* as agreed upon in the treaty
96 *unimprovèd mettle:* untested courage
97 *skirts:* borderlands
98 *sharked up a list:* drummed up troops (*Truppen ausgehoben*)
        lawless resolutes: men fighting for payment
100 *that hath a stomach in't:* who are ready to serve
         which is no other: which means nothing else
101 *as ... state:* as is only too clear to us
103 *terms compulsatory:* forced acceptance
         foresaid: mentioned earlier

And why such daily cast of brazen cannon
And foreign mart for implements of war;
75   Why such impress of shipwrights, whose sore task
Does not divide the Sunday from the week.
What might be toward, that this sweaty haste
Doth make the night joint-labourer with the day?
Who is't that can inform me?

HORATIO: That can I.
80   At least, the whisper goes so. Our last king,
Whose image even but now appeared to us,
Was, as you know, by Fortinbras of Norway,
Thereto pricked on by a most emulate pride,
Dared to the combat; in which our valiant Hamlet –
85   For so this side of our known world esteemed him –
Did slay this Fortinbras; who, by a sealed compact,
Well ratified by law and heraldry,
Did forfeit, with his life, all those his lands
Which he stood seized of, to the conqueror;
90   Against the which a moiety competent
Was gagèd by our king; which had returned
To the inheritance of Fortinbras,
Had he been vanquisher, as, by the same cov'nant
And carriage of the article designed,
95   His fell to Hamlet. Now, sir, young Fortinbras,
Of unimprovèd mettle hot and full,
Hath in the skirts of Norway, here and there,
Sharked up a list of lawless resolutes,
For food and diet, to some enterprise
100   That hath a stomach in't; which is no other,
As it doth well appear unto our state,
But to recover of us, by strong hand
And terms compulsatory, those foresaid lands
So by his father lost; and this, I take it,
105   Is the main motive of our preparations,

106 *source:* cause
   chief head: main reason, origin
107 *post-haste and romage:* hectic activity
108 *e'en so:* exactly this
109 *well may it sort:* it may well turn out
   portentous: threatening
111 *question:* cause
112 *mote:* tiny particle; irritant
113 *palmy:* glorious
114 *ere:* before
   Julius: Julius Caesar (100–44 BC, Roman general and statesman, publicly murdered)
115 *tenantless:* empty
   sheeted: wrapped in sheets
116 *squeak and gibber:* make high sounds and speak too quickly
117 *stars with trains of fire:* comets
   dews: Tau
118 *the moist star:* the moon
119 *Neptune's empire:* the ocean (Neptune is the Roman god of the sea)
120 *was … eclipse:* almost disappeared completely
121 *the like precurse:* the same feeling that sth. bad is going to happen
122 *harbinger:* forerunner, messenger
   preceding: coming before
123 *prologue:* introduction
125 *climatures:* territories
126 *soft:* wait a moment
   lo! (exclamation): look!
127 *cross* (v): confront
   though it blast me: even if it destroys me
131 *do ease:* remove a burden
   do grace: honour, show respect
133 *if thou art privy to:* if you have secret knowledge of
134 *foreknowing:* prior knowledge

The source of this our watch, and the chief head
Of this post-haste and romage in the land.
BARNARDO: I think it be no other but e'en so.
Well may it sort that this portentous figure
110   Comes armèd through our watch, so like the king
That was and is the question of these wars.
HORATIO: A mote it is to trouble the mind's eye.
In the most high and palmy state of Rome,
A little ere the mightiest Julius fell,
115   The graves stood tenantless, and the sheeted dead
Did squeak and gibber in the Roman streets;
As stars with trains of fire, and dews of blood,
Disasters in the sun; and the moist star
Upon whose influence Neptune's empire stands
120   Was sick almost to doomsday with eclipse.
And even the like precurse of fierce events,
As harbingers preceding still the fates
And prologue to the omen coming on,
Have heaven and earth together demonstrated
125   Unto our climatures and countrymen.

Enter GHOST *again.*

But soft! Behold! Lo, where it comes again!
I'll cross it, though it blast me. – Stay, illusion!

The GHOST spreads his arms.

If thou hast any sound, or use of voice,
Speak to me.
130   If there be any good thing to be done,
That may to thee do ease, and, grace to me,
Speak to me.
If thou art privy to thy country's fate,
Which happily foreknowing may avoid,

136 *uphoarded:* collected in great quantity and hidden
137 *extorted:* got by evil means
       womb [wu:m]: belly
140 *partisan:* long spear with an axe-head
141 *stand:* stop before them
145 *invulnerable:* impossible to hurt
146 *vain blows:* useless attempts to hit it
       malicious mockery: wicked, evil-minded ridicule
149 *a fearful summons:* an order to appear that it was afraid of
150 *morn:* morning
151 *lofty:* high-sounding
154 *extravagant and erring:* wandering
154–155 *hies to his confine:* hurries to his prison
155 *herein:* of this
156 *present object:* i.e. the ghost
       made probation: gave proof
158 *ever 'gainst:* always before
159 *our Saviour:* Jesus Christ
160 *bird of dawning:* cock
161 *dare stir:* is bold enough to move

135 O, speak!
Or if thou hast uphoarded in thy life
Extorted treasure in the womb of earth
For which, they say, you spirits oft walk in death.

The cock crows.

Speak of it! Stay, and speak! Stop it, Marcellus!
140 **MARCELLUS:** Shall I strike at it with my partisan?
HORATIO: Do, if it will not stand.
BARNARDO: 'Tis here!
HORATIO: 'Tis here!
MARCELLUS: 'Tis gone!

Exit GHOST.

We do it wrong, being so majestical,
To offer it the show of violence;
145 For it is as the air, invulnerable,
And our vain blows malicious mockery.
BARNARDO: It was about to speak, when the cock crew.
HORATIO: And then it started, like a guilty thing
Upon a fearful summons. I have heard
150 The cock, that is the trumpet to the morn,
Doth with his lofty and shrill-sounding throat
Awake the god of day; and at his warning,
Whether in sea or fire, in earth or air,
Th' extravagant and erring spirit hies
155 To his confine; and of the truth herein
This present object made probation.
MARCELLUS: It faded on the crowing of the cock.
Some say that ever 'gainst that season comes
Wherein our Saviour's birth is celebrated,
160 The bird of dawning singeth all night long;
And then, they say, no spirit dare stir abroad,

162 *wholesome:* fine, healthy
    strike: have an evil influence
163 *no fairy takes:* no elf does harm
    charm: use magic
164 *hallowed:* holy
    gracious: kind; full of divine grace
166 *in russet mantle clad:* dressed in a reddish covering
167 *dew:* morning dampness
    yon ...: this ... over there
169 *impart:* tell
171 *dumb:* not speaking, silent
172 *consent:* agree
    acquaint him with it: inform him
173 *as needful in our loves:* what we owe each other as brothers
175 *conveniently:* easily

The nights are wholesome, then no planets strike,
No fairy takes, nor witch hath power to charm,
So hallowed and so gracious is the time.
165 **HORATIO:** So have I heard and do in part believe it.
But look, the morn, in russet mantle clad,
Walks o'er the dew of yon high eastward hill.
Break we our watch up; and by my advice
Let us impart what we have seen tonight
170 Unto young Hamlet; for, upon my life,
This spirit, dumb to us, will speak to him.
Do you consent we shall acquaint him with it,
As needful in our loves, fitting our duty?
MARCELLUS: Let's do't, I pray; and I this morning know
175 Where we shall find him most conveniently.

Exeunt.

Summary:

In the Great Hall of Elsinore Castle, King Claudius of Denmark informs the court that, despite his grief for his brother's death, he has married Old Hamlet's widow, Queen Gertrude. Claudius sends two ambassadors to make peace with the King of Norway, whose nephew, Prince Fortinbras, has threatened to retake land which the Danes had won from the Norwegians. When Laertes, Lord Chamberlain Polonius's son, asks permission to return to France after the coronation, Claudius grants it. He and Gertrude criticize young Hamlet for still grieving for his dead father after two months. Both ask Hamlet to stay at court and not to take up his studies in Wittenberg again, which he promises his mother even though he is deeply offended by her quick remarriage. Horatio and the Watch inform Hamlet that they have repeatedly seen Old Hamlet's ghost at midnight. The prince urges them not to reveal what they have seen and arranges to join them on watch the following night.

Annotations:

1–2 *though ... green:* although the memory is still fresh
Hamlet: the former King of Denmark, Hamlet's father
2 *befitted:* was fitting, appropriate
4 *contracted in one brow of woe:* grieving
5 *discretion* [dɪˈskreʃn]: common sense
6 *wisest sorrow:* mourning checked by sound judgement
7 *with remembrance of ourselves:* with regard to those living
8 *sometime:* former
9 *imperial jointress:* i.e. Gertrude ruling with him as the former king's wife
warlike: militarily well prepared
10 *as 'twere:* as is the case
defeated: subdued, restrained
11 *auspicious:* full of hopeful promise
dropping: sorrowful
12 *mirth:* cheerfulness
dirge: funeral song
13 *in equal scale:* well balanced
dole: sadness
14 *barred:* disregarded
15 *wisdoms:* knowledge
18 *weak supposal:* poor opinion
worth: power, excellence
20 *disjoint and out of frame:* lacking law and order, falling to pieces
21 *colleaguèd:* combined
22 *pester:* molest, anger
23 *importing:* concerning
surrender: giving up
24 *bands of law:* lawfully binding obligations
25 *valiant:* brave

Scene II

Elsinore. A room of state in the castle.

Flourish. Enter CLAUDIUS, THE KING OF DENMARK, THE QUEEN, HAMLET, POLONIUS, LAERTES *and his sister* OPHELIA, VOLTEMAND, CORNELIUS, LORDS *attendant.*

CLAUDIUS: Though yet of Hamlet our dear brother's death
  The memory be green, and that it us befitted
  To bear our hearts in grief, and our whole kingdom
  To be contracted in one brow of woe,
5 Yet so far hath discretion fought with nature
  That we with wisest sorrow think on him
  Together with remembrance of ourselves.
  Therefore our sometime sister, now our queen,
  Th' imperial jointress to this warlike state,
10 Have we, as 'twere with a defeated joy,
  With an auspicious, and a dropping eye,
  With mirth in funeral, and with dirge in marriage,
  In equal scale weighing delight and dole,
  Taken to wife; nor have we herein barred
15 Your better wisdoms, which have freely gone
  With this affair along. For all, our thanks.
  Now follows, that you know: young Fortinbras,
  Holding a weak supposal of our worth,
  Or thinking by our late dear brother's death
20 Our state to be disjoint and out of frame,
  Colleaguèd with this dream of his advantage,
  He hath not failed to pester us with message
  Importing the surrender of those lands
  Lost by his father, with all bands of law,
25 To our most valiant brother. So much for him.
  Now for ourself and for this time of meeting.
  Thus much the business is: we have here writ

28 *Norway:* King of Norway
29 *impotent:* powerless
     bed-rid: confined to his bed
30 *purpose:* ambition
     suppress: keep in check
31 *his further gait herein:* Fortinbras's going ahead with his plans
     in that: because
31/32 *levies/lists:* soldiers
32 *full proportions:* full number of soldiers
     made: taken
33 *subject:* people
     dispatch: send away
36–37 *power to business:* authority to do business
37 *scope:* room
38 *dilated articles:* detailed statements
39 *commend:* tell of
41 *nothing:* not at all
43 *suit:* formal request
44–45 *speak … voice:* have a good reason for your request
44 *the Dane:* the Danish king, i.e. Claudius
46 *that … asking:* which I could not grant or you could not ask for
47 *native:* closely related
48 *instrumental:* useful
50 *dread:* highly respected
51 *leave and favour:* permission
52 *from whence:* from where
55 *bend* (v): turn
56 *bow:* submit

To Norway, uncle of young Fortinbras,
Who, impotent and bed-rid, scarcely hears
30 Of this his nephew's purpose, to suppress
His further gait herein, in that the levies,
The lists, and full proportions are all made
Out of his subject; and we here dispatch
You, good Cornelius, and you, Voltemand,
35 For bearers of this greeting to old Norway,
Giving to you no further personal power
To business with the king, more than the scope
Of these dilated articles allow. *[Gives a paper.]*
Farewell, and let your haste commend your duty.

CORNELIUS: ⎫ In that, and all things, will we show our duty.
40 **VOLTEMAND:** ⎭

CLAUDIUS: We doubt it nothing. Heartily farewell.

Exeunt VOLTEMAND *and* CORNELIUS.

And now, Laertes, what's the news with you?
You told us of some suit. What is't, Laertes?
You cannot speak of reason to the Dane
45 And lose your voice. What wouldst thou beg, Laertes,
That shall not be my offer, not thy asking?
The head is not more native to the heart,
The hand more instrumental to the mouth,
Than is the throne of Denmark to thy father.
50 What wouldst thou have, Laertes?

LAERTES: My dread lord,
Your leave and favour to return to France;
From whence though willingly I came to Denmark
To show my duty in your coronation,
Yet now I must confess, that duty done,
55 My thoughts and wishes bend again toward France
And bow them to your gracious leave and pardon.

CLAUDIUS: Have you your father's leave? What says Polonius?

58   *wrung:* got with difficulty
         slow: hesitant
59   *laboursome petition:* relentless asking
60   *sealed:* gave
         hard consent: reluctant agreement
61   *beseech:* urgently beg
62   *take thy fair hour:* make the most of your time
63   *thy best graces:* your best qualities/virtues
         at thy will: as you like
64   *cousin:* any close relative
65   *kin:* related, i.e. his stepson and nephew
         less than kind: not of your kind, less than familial
66   *clouds still hang on you:* you look unhappy
68   *cast thy nighted colour off:* take off your black clothes
69   *Denmark:* King Claudius
70   *vailèd lids:* eyes looking downwards
75   *particular:* personal
77   *inky:* black
78   *customary:* usual
79   *windy suspiration:* sighing
80   *fruitful river:* tears
81   *dejected:* depressed
         haviour of the visage: facial expression
83   *denote me truly:* indicate how I really feel
85   *passes show:* goes beyond mere show
86   *trappings and suits of woe:* elements proving his genuine grief
87   *commendable:* worthy of praise
90–91   *bound in filial obligation:* forced by a child's duty
91   *term:* time

POLONIUS: He hath, my lord, wrung from me my slow leave
    By laboursome petition, and at last
60   Upon his will I sealed my hard consent.
    I do beseech you give him leave to go.
CLAUDIUS: Take thy fair hour, Laertes. Time be thine,
    And thy best graces spend it at thy will!
    But now, my cousin Hamlet, and my son –
65 **HAMLET:** *[Aside]* A little more than kin, and less than kind.
CLAUDIUS: How is it that the clouds still hang on you?
HAMLET: Not so, my lord. I am too much i' th' sun.
GERTRUDE: Good Hamlet, cast thy nighted colour off,
    And let thine eye look like a friend on Denmark.
70   Do not for ever with thy vailèd lids
    Seek for thy noble father in the dust.
    Thou know'st 'tis common. All that lives must die,
    Passing through nature to eternity.
HAMLET: Ay, madam, it is common.
GERTRUDE: If it be,
75   Why seems it so particular with thee?
HAMLET: Seems, madam? Nay, it is. I know not 'seems'.
    'Tis not alone my inky cloak, good mother,
    Nor customary suits of solemn black,
    Nor windy suspiration of forced breath,
80   No, nor the fruitful river in the eye,
    Nor the dejected haviour of the visage,
    Together with all forms, moods, shapes of grief,
    That can denote me truly. These indeed seem,
    For they are actions that a man might play;
85   But I have that within which passes show –
    These but the trappings and the suits of woe.
CLAUDIUS: 'Tis sweet and commendable in your nature, Hamlet,
    To give these mourning duties to your father;
    But you must know, your father lost a father;
90   That father lost, lost his, and the survivor bound
    In filial obligation for some term

92 *obsequious:* devoted as the ritual expects it
      persever: go on; persevere
93 *obstinate condolement:* stubborn mourning
94 *impious:* sinful
95 *incorrect:* disobedient
96 *unfortified:* not strengthened
98–99 *for ... sense:* things have to be accepted as they are
100 *peevish:* stubborn
101 *fie:* exclamation of disgust
       fault: offence
104 *still:* always
105 *corse:* corpse
106 *pray:* beg
107 *unprevailing:* pointless
109 *the most immediate:* the next in line, heir to the throne

Note, l. 109: Denmark's monarchy was elective, i.e. the king was chosen by the
       nobility. With Hamlet away abroad in Germany and his marriage to his
       sister-in-law, Claudius managed to become king and not Hamlet, who is the
       lineal heir to the throne.

110 *nobility of love:* fatherly love
112 *impart:* offer
113 *Wittenberg:* German city well-known for its Protestant university
       retrograde: contrary
115 *bend you:* bring yourself to agree
116 *cheer and comfort of our eye:* our satisfaction
117 *chiefest:* most highly ranked
118 *lose her prayers:* pray in vain
121 *fair:* good
123 *gentle:* kind and noble
       accord: agreement
124 *sits smiling to my heart:* pleases me greatly
       in grace whereof: in regard to which
125 *jocund health:* toast in honour of

To do obsequious sorrow. But to persever
In obstinate condolement is a course
Of impious stubbornness. 'Tis unmanly grief;
It shows a will most incorrect to heaven,
A heart unfortified, a mind impatient,
An understanding simple and unschooled;
For what we know must be, and is as common
As any the most vulgar thing to sense,
Why should we in our peevish opposition
Take it to heart? Fie, 'tis a fault to heaven,
A fault against the dead, a fault to nature,
To reason most absurd, whose common theme
Is death of fathers, and who still hath cried,
From the first corse till he that died today,
'This must be so.' We pray you throw to earth
This unprevailing woe, and think of us
As of a father; for let the world take note
You are the most immediate to our throne,
And with no less nobility of love
Than that which dearest father bears his son
Do I impart toward you. For your intent
In going back to school in Wittenberg,
It is most retrograde to our desire;
And we beseech you, bend you to remain
Here in the cheer and comfort of our eye,
Our chiefest courtier, cousin, and our son.
GERTRUDE: Let not thy mother lose her prayers, Hamlet.
I pray thee stay with us, go not to Wittenberg.
HAMLET: I shall in all my best obey you, madam.
CLAUDIUS: Why, 'tis a loving and a fair reply.
Be as ourself in Denmark. Madam, come.
This gentle and unforced accord of Hamlet
Sits smiling to my heart; in grace whereof,
No jocund health that Denmark drinks today
But the great cannon to the clouds shall tell,

127   *rouse:* drinking a full draught of liquor
          bruit: announce with noise

Note, l. 127: It was then customary in Denmark to fire cannons during royal
celebrations. Some actors in Shakespeare's theatre company had performed
at Kronborg Castle in Elsinore (= Helsingør) and must have told him about
this ritual.

128   *re-speaking:* repeating
129   *solid:* firm, hard

Note, l. 129: In other print editions, the words 'sullied' (stained, dirtied) or
'sallied' (attacked) are used instead.

130   *thaw:* melt
          resolve: dissolve
131   *the Everlasting:* God
131–132   *fixed his canon:* set as permanent law
132   *self-slaughter:* suicide
133   *stale:* tasteless
          unprofitable: useless
134   *uses:* habits; practices
135   *unweeded:* not cleared of plants growing wild
136   *seed:* produce new plants
          rank and gross: foul and plentiful
137   *possess it merely:* take it up completely
140   *Hyperion:* byname of Helios, Greek god of the sun
          satyr: mythological creature with a great sexual appetite, half man, half goat
141   *beteem:* allow
146   *frailty:* weakness in a moral sense
147   *or ere:* before
149   *Niobe* ['naɪəbi]: ancient Greek queen constantly weeping for her dead
          children
150   *wants discourse of reason:* lacks intelligence
153   *Hercules:* hero from Greek mythology with super-human strength
154   *unrighteous:* false
155   *flushing:* redness
          gallèd: sore from crying
156   *wicked:* immoral
          post: hurry
157   *dexterity:* speed
          incestuous: involving sex between two closely related family members

And the king's rouse the heaven shall bruit again,
Re-speaking earthly thunder. Come away.

Flourish. Exeunt all but HAMLET.

HAMLET: O that this too too solid flesh would melt,
130   Thaw, and resolve itself into a dew,
Or that the Everlasting had not fixed
His canon 'gainst self-slaughter! O God! God!
How weary, stale, flat, and unprofitable
Seem to me all the uses of this world!
135   Fie on't, ah, fie! 'Tis an unweeded garden
That grows to seed; things rank and gross in nature
Possess it merely. That it should come to this!
But two months dead! Nay, not so much, not two.
So excellent a king, that was to this
140   Hyperion to a satyr; so loving to my mother
That he might not beteem the winds of heaven
Visit her face too roughly. Heaven and earth!
Must I remember? Why, she would hang on him
As if increase of appetite had grown
145   By what it fed on; and yet, within a month –
Let me not think on't! Frailty, thy name is woman!
A little month, or ere those shoes were old
With which she followed my poor father's body
Like Niobe, all tears – why she, even she –
150   O God! A beast that wants discourse of reason
Would have mourned longer – married with my uncle;
My father's brother, but no more like my father
Than I to Hercules. Within a month,
Ere yet the salt of most unrighteous tears
155   Had left the flushing in her gallèd eyes,
She married. O, most wicked speed, to post
With such dexterity to incestuous sheets!

160 *hail:* form of greeting
163 *change ... you:* call you 'friend'
164 *what make you from:* what are you doing away from
167 *even:* evening, also used for the afternoon
168 *in faith:* actually
169 *truant disposition:* lazy nature
172 *truster:* believer
173 *truant:* sb. who neglects his duties
174 *affair:* business
179 *hard upon:* quickly
180 *thrift:* habit of spending little money
    baked meats: meat pies
181 *did coldly furnish forth:* were served as cold dishes
182 *dearest foe:* greatest enemy
183 *or ever:* before

It is not, nor it cannot come to good.
But break my heart, for I must hold my tongue!

Enter HORATIO, MARCELLUS, *and* BARNARDO.

160 **HORATIO:** Hail to your lordship!
HAMLET: I am glad to see you well.
   Horatio! Or I do forget myself.
HORATIO: The same, my lord, and your poor servant ever.
HAMLET: Sir, my good friend – I'll change that name with you.
   And what make you from Wittenberg, Horatio?
165   Marcellus?
MARCELLUS: My good lord!
HAMLET: I am very glad to see you. *[To* BARNARDO*]* Good even, sir.
   But what, in faith, make you from Wittenberg?
HORATIO: A truant disposition, good my lord.
170 **HAMLET:** I would not hear your enemy say so,
   Nor shall you do my ear that violence
   To make it truster of your own report
   Against yourself. I know you are no truant.
   But what is your affair in Elsinore?
175   We'll teach you to drink deep ere you depart.
HORATIO: My lord, I came to see your father's funeral.
HAMLET: I prithee do not mock me, fellow student.
   I think it was to see my mother's wedding.
HORATIO: Indeed, my lord, it followed hard upon.
180 **HAMLET:** Thrift, thrift, Horatio! The funeral baked meats
   Did coldly furnish forth the marriage tables.
   Would I had met my dearest foe in heaven
   Or ever I had seen that day, Horatio!
   My father- methinks I see my father.
185 **HORATIO:** O, where, my lord?
HAMLET: In my mind's eye, Horatio.
HORATIO: I saw him once. He was a goodly king.

187 *all in all:* considering all his qualities
189 *yesternight:* last night
192 *season your admiration:* control your astonishment
193 *attent:* carefully listening
     deliver: report
194 *upon the witness:* with the confirmation
195 *marvel:* miracle
198 *dead waste:* desolate space
200 *at point:* correct in every detail
     cap-à-pie: from top to toe
201 *solemn:* serious
202 *stately:* full of dignity
     thrice: three times
203 *oppressed and fear-surprisèd:* troubled and afraid
204 *truncheon:* wooden military staff
     distilled: melted
205 *jelly: Gelee*
     act (n): influence
207 *dreadful:* full of fear
     impart: make known
209 *delivered:* described
213 *platform:* terrace with mounted guns
216–217 *did address itself to motion:* began to move

HAMLET: He was a man, take him for all in all.
I shall not look upon his like again.
HORATIO: My lord, I think I saw him yesternight.
190 **HAMLET:** Saw? Who?
HORATIO: My lord, the king your father.
HAMLET: The king my father?
HORATIO: Season your admiration for a while
With an attent ear, till I may deliver
Upon the witness of these gentlemen,
195 This marvel to you.
HAMLET: For God's love let me hear!
HORATIO: Two nights together had these gentlemen,
Marcellus and Barnardo, on their watch
In the dead waste and middle of the night
Been thus encountered. A figure like your father,
200 Armèd at point exactly, cap-à-pie,
Appears before them and with solemn march
Goes slow and stately by them. Thrice he walked
By their oppressed and fear-surprisèd eyes,
Within his truncheon's length; whilst they distilled
205 Almost to jelly with the act of fear,
Stand dumb and speak not to him. This to me
In dreadful secrecy impart they did,
And I with them the third night kept the watch;
Where, as they had delivered, both in time,
210 Form of the thing, each word made true and good,
The apparition comes. I knew your father.
These hands are not more like.
HAMLET: But where was this?
MARCELLUS: My lord, upon the platform where we watched.
HAMLET: Did you not speak to it?
HORATIO: My lord, I did;
215 But answer made it none. Yet once methought
It lifted up its head and did address
Itself to motion, like as it would speak;

218 *crew:* crowed
219 *shrunk in haste away:* disappeared quickly
222 *writ down:* laid down
225 *hold you the watch:* are you on guard duty
230 *beaver:* movable part of a helmet covering the face
232 *countenance:* facial expression
238 *tell:* count
240 *grizzled:* greyish
242 *sable silvered:* black mixed with grey

But even then the morning cock crew loud,
And at the sound it shrunk in haste away
220 And vanished from our sight.

HAMLET: 'Tis very strange.

HORATIO: As I do live, my honoured lord, 'tis true;
And we did think it writ down in our duty
To let you know of it.

HAMLET: Indeed, indeed, sirs. But this troubles me.
225 Hold you the watch tonight?

MARCELLUS: }
BARNARDO: } We do, my lord.

HAMLET: Armed, say you?

MARCELLUS: }
BARNARDO: } Armed, my lord.

HAMLET: From top to toe?

MARCELLUS: }
BARNARDO: } My lord, from head to foot.

HAMLET: Then saw you not his face?

230 **HORATIO:** O, yes, my lord! He wore his beaver up.

HAMLET: What, looked he frowningly?

HORATIO: A countenance more in sorrow than in anger.

HAMLET: Pale or red?

HORATIO: Nay, very pale.

HAMLET: And fixed his eyes upon you?

235 **HORATIO:** Most constantly.

HAMLET: I would I had been there.

HORATIO: It would have much amazed you.

HAMLET: Very like, very like. Stayed it long?

HORATIO: While one with moderate haste might tell a hundred.

MARCELLUS: }
BARNARDO: } Longer, longer.

240 **HORATIO:** Not when I saw't.

HAMLET: His beard was grizzled – no?

HORATIO: It was, as I have seen it in his life,
A sable silvered.

243 *perchance:* perhaps
    I warrant: I assure you
244 *assume:* takes on
245 *gape:* scream
246 *hold my peace:* be quiet
247 *hitherto:* so far
    concealed: kept secret
248 *tenable:* retained
249 *whatsomever:* whatever
    hap: happen
250 *give ... tongue:* be aware of it but don't say anything
251 *requite your loves:* reward your favour
252 *'twixt:* between
256 *doubt:* suspect
258 *though ... eyes:* however deeply they are buried

HAMLET: I will watch tonight.
　　Perchance 'twill walk again.
HORATIO: I warrant it will.
HAMLET: If it assume my noble father's person,
245　I'll speak to it, though hell itself should gape
　　And bid me hold my peace. I pray you all,
　　If you have hitherto concealed this sight,
　　Let it be tenable in your silence still;
　　And whatsomever else shall hap tonight,
250　Give it an understanding but no tongue.
　　I will requite your loves. So, fare you well.
　　Upon the platform, 'twixt eleven and twelve,
　　I'll visit you.
ALL: Our duty to your honour.
HAMLET: Your loves, as mine to you. Farewell.

Exeunt all but HAMLET.

255　My father's spirit in arms? All is not well.
　　I doubt some foul play. Would the night were come!
　　Till then sit still, my soul. Foul deeds will rise,
　　Though all the earth o'erwhelm them, to men's eyes.

Exit.

Summary:

In a private room and preparing to leave for France, Laertes warns his sister Ophelia not to pay attention to Hamlet's advances because his marriage will be a politically arranged one. Laertes advises her not to fall in love with the prince because young people can be reckless. Ophelia suggests he should listen to his own advice too. Polonius enters to hurry his son and gives him detailed advice on how to behave abroad. Alone with Ophelia, Polonius questions her about her meetings with Hamlet and orders her to stop seeing him with the same arguments Laertes used. Ophelia is not convinced that her relatives need to worry about Hamlet's behaviour, but agrees to stay away from him.

Annotations:

1 *necessaries:* personal luggage
   embarked: on the ship
2 *as:* whenever
   give benefit: are favourable
3 *convoy is assistant:* ships are ready
5 *trifling of his favour:* foolish behaviour
6 *hold it a fashion:* take it for a passing mood
   toy in blood: childish fancy
7 *the youth of primy nature:* in its prime, early
8 *forward:* enthusiastic, wilful
9 *suppliance:* pleasurable pastime
10 *but so:* than that
11 *crescent* [ˈkresnt]: growing
12 *in thews and bulk:* in physical strength
   temple waxes: body grows
13 *inward service:* inner workings
14 *withal:* at the same time
15 *no soil nor cautel:* no stain nor dishonesty
   besmirch: make dirty
16 *virtue of his will:* purity of his intention
19 *unvalued:* ordinary
20 *carve:* choose
21 *sanctity:* worthiness
22 *circumscribed:* restricted
23 *the voice and yielding of that body:* the vote and consent of that nation
24 *whereof:* of which
26 *particular act and place:* particular rank and power

Scene III

Elsinore. A room in the house of POLONIUS.

Enter LAERTES *and* OPHELIA.

LAERTES: My necessaries are embarked. Farewell.
    And, sister, as the winds give benefit
    And convoy is assistant, do not sleep,
    But let me hear from you.
OPHELIA: Do you doubt that?
5 **LAERTES:** For Hamlet, and the trifling of his favour,
    Hold it a fashion, and a toy in blood;
    A violet in the youth of primy nature,
    Forward, not permanent – sweet, not lasting;
    The perfume and suppliance of a minute;
10   No more.
OPHELIA: No more but so?
LAERTES: Think it no more.
    For nature crescent does not grow alone
    In thews and bulk; but as this temple waxes,
    The inward service of the mind and soul
    Grows wide withal. Perhaps he loves you now,
15   And now no soil nor cautel doth besmirch
    The virtue of his will; but you must fear,
    His greatness weighed, his will is not his own;
    For he himself is subject to his birth.
    He may not, as unvalued persons do,
20   Carve for himself, for on his choice depends
    The sanctity and health of this whole state,
    And therefore must his choice be circumscribed
    Unto the voice and yielding of that body
    Whereof he is the head. Then if he says he loves you,
25   It fits your wisdom so far to believe it
    As he in his particular act and place

27   *give his saying deed:* make him act according to his words
28   *main voice:* opinion of the majority
29   *sustain:* suffer
30   *credent:* trusting
        list his songs: listen to his talk of love
31   *chaste treasure:* virginity
32   *unmastered importunity:* uncontrolled urgency
34   *keep you in the rear of your affection:* hold yourself back
36   *chariest maid:* very modest virgin
        prodigal: generous
38   *'scapes:* escapes
        calumnious strokes: slanderous attacks
39   *canker:* disease that damages or destroys plants
        galls: injures, destroys
        infants: young plants and flowers
40   *buttons be disclosed:* flower buds open
41   *liquid dew of youth:* morning dampness
42   *contagious blastments:* infectious diseases
        imminent: likely to happen soon
43   *wary:* careful
45   *effect:* importance
47   *ungracious:* ungodly
49   *puffed and reckless:* vain and careless
        libertine: pleasure seeker
50   *the primrose path of dalliance treads:* delights in every chance of behaving
        immorally
51   *recks not his own rede:* ignores his own advice
52   *fear me not:* do not worry about me
55   *occasion smiles upon a second leave:* it is favourable to say goodbye again
58   *you are stayed for:* they are waiting for you

May give his saying deed; which is no further
Than the main voice of Denmark goes withal.
Then weigh what loss your honour may sustain
30   If with too credent ear you list his songs,
Or lose your heart, or your chaste treasure open
To his unmastered importunity.
Fear it, Ophelia, fear it, my dear sister,
And keep you in the rear of your affection,
35   Out of the shot and danger of desire.
The chariest maid is prodigal enough
If she unmask her beauty to the moon.
Virtue itself 'scapes not calumnious strokes.
The canker galls the infants of the spring
40   Too oft before their buttons be disclosed,
And in the morn and liquid dew of youth
Contagious blastments are most imminent.
Be wary then; best safety lies in fear.
Youth to itself rebels, though none else near.
45 **OPHELIA:** I shall th' effect of this good lesson keep
As watchman to my heart. But, good my brother,
Do not as some ungracious pastors do,
Show me the steep and thorny way to heaven,
Whiles, like a puffed and reckless libertine,
50   Himself the primrose path of dalliance treads
And recks not his own rede.
LAERTES: O, fear me not!

Enter POLONIUS.

I stay too long. But here my father comes.
A double blessing is a double grace;
55   Occasion smiles upon a second leave.
POLONIUS: Yet here, Laertes? Aboard, aboard, for shame!
The wind sits in the shoulder of your sail,
And you are stayed for. There – my blessing with thee!

59   *precepts:* moral lessons
60   *look thou character:* see that you remember
61   *unproportioned:* disorderly
62   *familiar:* friendly
63   *adoption tried:* friendship tested
64   *grapple:* fasten
          hoops: circular bands
65   *do not dull thy palm:* do not shake hands too often
66   *new-hatched:* recent
          unfledged: young, untried
          courage: mate, comrade
68   *bear't ... opposèd:* manage it so that your opponent
70   *censure:* opinion
71   *habit:* clothes
72   *fancy:* extravagance
          gaudy: showy
73   *the apparel oft proclaims the man:* clothing often declares who one is
75   *are ... that:* are particularly known for their good taste in clothes
78   *dulls the edge of husbandry:* leads one to spend more money than one should
82   *season this in thee:* shall enrich what I have told you
84   *tend:* are ready to serve

And these few precepts in thy memory
60 Look thou character. Give thy thoughts no tongue,
Nor any unproportioned thought his act.
Be thou familiar, but by no means vulgar:
Those friends thou hast, and their adoption tried,
Grapple them unto thy soul with hoops of steel;
65 But do not dull thy palm with entertainment
Of each new-hatched, unfledged courage. Beware
Of entrance to a quarrel; but being in,
Bear't that th'opposèd may beware of thee.
Give every man thine ear, but few thy voice;
70 Take each man's censure, but reserve thy judgement.
Costly thy habit as thy purse can buy,
But not expressed in fancy; rich, not gaudy;
For the apparel oft proclaims the man,
And they in France of the best rank and station
75 Are of a most select and generous chief in that.
Neither a borrower nor a lender be;
For loan oft loses both itself and friend,
And borrowing dulls the edge of husbandry.
This above all – to thine own self be true,
80 And it must follow, as the night the day,
Thou canst not then be false to any man.
Farewell. My blessing season this in thee!
LAERTES: Most humbly do I take my leave, my lord.
POLONIUS: The time invites you. Go, your servants tend.
85 **LAERTES:** Farewell, Ophelia, and remember well
What I have said to you.
OPHELIA: 'Tis in my memory locked,
And you yourself shall keep the key of it.
LAERTES: Farewell.

Exit.

POLONIUS: What is't, Ophelia, he hath said to you?

91 *marry:* by the Virgin Mary
    bethought: thought of
94 *audience:* time
    bounteous: open-hearted, generous
95 *put on me:* given me to understand
96 *caution:* warning
98 *behooves:* becomes
100 *tenders:* offers
102 *green:* inexperienced
103 *unsifted:* immature; not tested
    perilous ['perələs]: dangerous
107 *ta'en:* taken
108 *sterling:* of true value, genuine
    tender: regard
109 *crack the wind of:* weaken
111 *importuned:* addressed
113 *go to, go to!:* enough of this!
114 *countenance:* authority, strength
116 *springes:* traps
    woodcocks: type of birds (*Waldschnepfe*) thought to be foolish then
117 *prodigal:* freely
118 *blazes:* flaring flames
119 *extinct:* put out
120 *as it is a-making:* even while it is said
122 *scanter:* less free
123 *entreatments:* discussions
124 *command to parley:* invitation to talk about love

90 **OPHELIA:** So please you, something touching the Lord Hamlet.
  POLONIUS: Marry, well bethought!
      'Tis told me he hath very oft of late
      Given private time to you, and you yourself
      Have of your audience been most free and bounteous.
95   If it be so – as so 'tis put on me,
      And that in way of caution I must tell you
      You do not understand yourself so clearly
      As it behooves my daughter and your honour.
      What is between you? Give me up the truth.
100 **OPHELIA:** He hath, my lord, of late made many tenders
      Of his affection to me.
  POLONIUS: Affection? Pooh! You speak like a green girl,
      Unsifted in such perilous circumstance.
      Do you believe his tenders, as you call them?
105 **OPHELIA:** I do not know, my lord, what I should think.
  POLONIUS: Marry, I will teach you! Think yourself a baby
      That you have ta'en these tenders for true pay,
      Which are not sterling. Tender yourself more dearly,
      Or not to crack the wind of the poor phrase,
110   Running it thus you'll tender me a fool.
  OPHELIA: My lord, he hath importuned me with love
      In honourable fashion.
  POLONIUS: Ay, fashion you may call it. Go to, go to!
  OPHELIA: And hath given countenance to his speech, my lord,
115   With almost all the holy vows of heaven.
  POLONIUS: Ay, springes to catch woodcocks! I do know,
      When the blood burns, how prodigal the soul
      Lends the tongue vows. These blazes, daughter,
      Giving more light than heat, extinct in both
120   Even in their promise, as it is a-making,
      You must not take for fire. From this time
      Be something scanter of your maiden presence.
      Set your entreatments at a higher rate
      Than a command to parley. For Lord Hamlet,

126 *larger tether:* longer rope
127 *in few:* in short
128 *brokers:* traders, go-betweens
129 *dye:* colour
    investments: clothes
130 *implorators of unholy suits:* those who request immoral acts
131 *sanctified and pious bonds:* holy, religious duties; marriage vows
132 *beguile* [bɪˈgaɪl]: deceive
    for all: in sum
134 *slander:* bring shame upon
136 *look to't:* be on your guard
    charge (v): order
    come your ways: come along

125   Believe so much in him, that he is young,
        And with a larger tether may he walk
        Than may be given you. In few, Ophelia,
        Do not believe his vows; for they are brokers,
        Not of that dye which their investments show,
130   But mere implorators of unholy suits,
        Breathing like sanctified and pious bonds,
        The better to beguile. This is for all:
        I would not, in plain terms, from this time forth
        Have you so slander any moment leisure
135   As to give words or talk with the Lord Hamlet.
        Look to't, I charge you. Come your ways.
OPHELIA: I shall obey, my lord.

Exeunt.

Summary:

On watch with Horatio and the soldiers at midnight, Hamlet sees his father's ghost, which beckons him away from the others. After they have unsuccessfully tried to hold Hamlet back, the men decide to follow Hamlet, who is determined to speak to the apparition.

Annotations:

1   *shrewdly:* sharply
2   *nipping; eager:* biting cold
4   *it lacks of twelve:* it is shortly before 12 o'clock
6   *held his wont* [wəʊnt] *to walk:* took his usual walk
      two pieces go off (stage direction): two cannons fire (cf. I, ii, 126)
8   *wake:* stay up
      takes his rouse: drinks, celebrates
9   *keeps wassail* [ˈwɒseɪl]: drinks and festivities
      swaggering upspring reels: wild and drunk dancing
10 *drains his draughts:* empties his drinking mugs
      Rhenish [ˈrenɪʃ]: from Germany's Rhineland
11 *kettle-drum:* percussion instrument
      bray out: roar loudly
12 *pledge:* toast
15 *to the manner born:* used to this custom
16 *breach:* breaking of it
      observance: keeping the practice
17 *revel:* festivity
18 *traduced and taxed of:* defamed and criticized by
19 *clepe:* call
20 *soil our addition:* slander our name
22 *pith; marrow: Knochenmark*
      pith and marrow of our attribute: our good reputation
23 *chances:* happens
24 *vicious:* morally corrupt
      mole of nature: negative character trait (*mole = Muttermal*)

Scene IV

Elsinore. The platform before the castle.

Enter HAMLET, HORATIO, *and* MARCELLUS.

HAMLET: The air bites shrewdly; it is very cold.
HORATIO: It is a nipping and an eager air.
HAMLET: What hour now?
HORATIO: I think it lacks of twelve.
MARCELLUS: No, it is struck.
5 **HORATIO:** Indeed? I heard it not. It then draws near the season
    Wherein the spirit held his wont to walk.

A flourish of trumpets, and two pieces go off.

    What does this mean, my lord?
HAMLET: The king doth wake tonight and takes his rouse,
    Keeps wassail, and the swaggering upspring reels,
10   And, as he drains his draughts of Rhenish down,
    The kettle-drum and trumpet thus bray out
    The triumph of his pledge.
HORATIO: Is it a custom?
HAMLET: Ay, marry, is't;
    But to my mind, though I am native here
15   And to the manner born, it is a custom
    More honoured in the breach than the observance.
    This heavy-headed revel east and west
    Makes us traduced and taxed of other nations;
    They clepe us drunkards and with swinish phrase
20   Soil our addition; and indeed it takes
    From our achievements, though performed at height,
    The pith and marrow of our attribute.
    So oft it chances in particular men
    That, for some vicious mole of nature in them,

27 *o'ergrowth of some complexion:* excessive character flaw
28 *pales and forts:* boundaries, fortified places
29–30 *o'erleavens the form of plausive manners:* influences decent behaviour
31 *stamp:* identifying mark, imprint
32 *nature's livery:* outward appearance, sth. they are born with
      fortune's star: sth. their fate leads them to
34 *infinite:* endless
      undergo: experience
35 *general censure:* public opinion
36 *dram:* small amount
36–38 *the dram ... scandal:* one small fault can ruin a good reputation
39 *ministers of grace:* angels
40 *spirit of health:* good spirit from heaven
      goblin damned: demon from hell
41 *airs; blasts:* breezes; strong movements of air
42 *intents:* aims, intentions
      charitable: kind
43 *questionable:* friendly, inviting questions
46 *burst in ignorance:* impatient for want of knowledge
47 *canonized:* buried according to ritual
      hearsèd: put into a coffin or grave
48 *burst their cerements:* torn their clothes for the grave
      sepulchre: tomb
49 *inurned:* buried
50 *oped:* opened
      ponderous: heavy
      marble (attr): Marmor-
      jaw: mouth and teeth of a person or an animal
51 *cast thee up:* throw you out of
52 *corse:* corpse
53 *glimpses of the moon:* moonlight
54 *hideous:* frightening
      fools of nature: ignorant mortal beings
55 *shake our disposition:* stir us with fear

25   As in their birth, – wherein they are not guilty,
     Since nature cannot choose his origin, –
     By the o'ergrowth of some complexion,
     Oft breaking down the pales and forts of reason,
     Or by some habit that too much o'erleavens
30   The form of plausive manners, that these men
     Carrying, I say, the stamp of one defect,
     Being nature's livery, or fortune's star,
     Their virtues else – be they as pure as grace,
     As infinite as man may undergo –
35   Shall in the general censure take corruption
     From that particular fault. The dram of e'il
     Doth all the noble substance often doubt
     To his own scandal.

Enter GHOST.

HORATIO: Look, my lord, it comes!
HAMLET: Angels and ministers of grace defend us!
40   Be thou a spirit of health or goblin damned,
     Bring with thee airs from heaven or blasts from hell,
     Be thy intents wicked or charitable,
     Thou com'st in such a questionable shape
     That I will speak to thee. I'll call thee Hamlet,
45   King, father, royal Dane. O, answer me.
     Let me not burst in ignorance, but tell
     Why thy canonized bones, hearsèd in death,
     Have burst their cerements; why the sepulchre
     Wherein we saw thee quietly inurned,
50   Hath oped his ponderous and marble jaws
     To cast thee up again. What may this mean
     That thou, dead corse, again in complete steel,
     Revisits thus the glimpses of the moon,
     Making night hideous, and we fools of nature
55   So horridly to shake our disposition

57   *wherefore:* why
  •   *beckons:* makes a sign to follow him
59   *impartment:* message
60   *courteous:* polite
61   *removèd ground:* remote place
65   *at a pin's fee:* worth of a pin; practically nothing
69   *flood:* sea
71   *beetles o'er:* overhangs
73   *deprive:* take away
       sovereignty of reason [ˈsɒvrənti]: rational thinking
75   *toys of desperation:* thoughts of suicide
77   *fathom:* measure of length (six feet)

With thoughts beyond the reaches of our souls?
Say, why is this? Wherefore? What should we do?

GHOST *beckons* HAMLET.

HORATIO: It beckons you to go away with it,
        As if it some impartment did desire
60   To you alone.
    MARCELLUS: Look with what courteous action
        It waves you to a more removèd ground.
        But do not go with it!
    HORATIO: No, by no means!
    HAMLET: It will not speak. Then will I follow it.
    HORATIO: Do not, my lord!
    HAMLET: Why, what should be the fear?
65   I do not set my life at a pin's fee;
        And for my soul, what can it do to that,
        Being a thing immortal as itself?
        It waves me forth again. I'll follow it.
    HORATIO: What if it tempt you toward the flood, my lord,
70   Or to the dreadful summit of the cliff
        That beetles o'er his base into the sea,
        And there assume some other, horrible form
        Which might deprive your sovereignty of reason
        And draw you into madness? Think of it.
75   The very place puts toys of desperation,
        Without more motive, into every brain
        That looks so many fathoms to the sea
        And hears it roar beneath.
    HAMLET: It waves me still. Go on. I'll follow thee.
80 **MARCELLUS:** You shall not go, my lord.
    HAMLET: Hold off your hands!
    HORATIO: Be ruled. You shall not go.

82   *petty arture:* little artery
83   *hardy:* strong
         Nemean lion: terrifying lion killed by Hercules (cf. I, ii, 153)
84   *unhand me:* let me go
85   *lets:* hinders
87   *waxes:* becomes more and more
89   *have after:* let's follow him
         issue: outcome

HAMLET: My fate cries out
And makes each petty arture in this body
As hardy as the Nemean lion's nerve.

GHOST *beckons.*

Still am I called. Unhand me, gentlemen.
85   By heaven, I'll make a ghost of him that lets me!
I say, away! Go on. I'll follow thee.

Exeunt GHOST *and* HAMLET.

HORATIO: He waxes desperate with imagination.
MARCELLUS: Let's follow. 'Tis not fit thus to obey him.
HORATIO: Have after. To what issue will this come?
90   **MARCELLUS:** Something is rotten in the state of Denmark.
HORATIO: Heaven will direct it.
MARCELLUS: Nay, let's follow him.

Exeunt.

Summary:

After introducing himself as Old Hamlet's ghost, the apparition tells Hamlet about his suffering in purgatory, a preliminary stage to hell, where he was sent because he couldn't confess his sins before death. This state can only be ended if Hamlet takes revenge on Old Hamlet's murderer Claudius, who poured poison into the sleeping king's ear in the garden. Though Claudius has now corrupted Hamlet's mother, Gertrude must not be harmed. Hamlet promises to act swiftly and the ghost departs at dawn. When Horatio and Marcellus join Hamlet, he makes them swear an oath on his sword never to disclose what happened, but does not give them any further information. He also tells them he might pretend to be insane and asks them not to let others know that Hamlet is not mad.

Annotations:

1 *whither:* whereto
2 *mark me:* listen to me
   my hour: daybreak
3 *sulph'rous: schweflig*
4 *render up:* give up
5 *lend thy serious hearing:* listen carefully
6 *unfold:* tell, reveal
   bound: ready; obliged
10 *doomed:* condemned
   term: period of time
11 *confined to fast:* kept from food
13 *purged:* cleansed, purified
   but: were it not
15 *lightest:* slightest, smallest
16 *harrow up:* fill with distress and fear
17 *start from their spheres:* jump from their fixed places

Note, l. 17: Stars and planets were thought to revolve around the earth in circles, each in their own sphere, creating the 'music of the spheres' in their movement which no human being could hear.

18 *knotted and combinèd locks:* neatly styled hair
20 *quills:* sharp, pointed spikes
   fretful: easily agitated
   porpentine: porcupine (*Stachelschwein*)
21 *eternal blazon:* telling of the afterlife
22 *list:* listen

Scene V

Elsinore. The castle. Another part of the fortifications.

Enter GHOST *and* HAMLET.

HAMLET: Whither wilt thou lead me? Speak! I'll go no further.
GHOST: Mark me.
HAMLET: I will.
GHOST: My hour is almost come,
    When I to sulph'rous and tormenting flames
    Must render up myself.
HAMLET: Alas, poor ghost!
5 **GHOST:** Pity me not, but lend thy serious hearing
    To what I shall unfold.
HAMLET: Speak. I am bound to hear.
GHOST: So art thou to revenge, when thou shalt hear.
HAMLET: What?
GHOST: I am thy father's spirit,
10   Doomed for a certain term to walk the night,
    And for the day confined to fast in fires,
    Till the foul crimes done in my days of nature
    Are burnt and purged away. But that I am forbid
    To tell the secrets of my prison house,
15   I could a tale unfold whose lightest word
    Would harrow up thy soul, freeze thy young blood,
    Make thy two eyes, like stars, start from their spheres,
    Thy knotted and combinèd locks to part,
    And each particular hair to stand on end
20   Like quills upon the fretful porpentine.
    But this eternal blazon must not be
    To ears of flesh and blood. List, list, O, list!
    If thou didst ever thy dear father love –
HAMLET: O God!
25 **GHOST:** Revenge his foul and most unnatural murder.

27	*as in the best it is:* even if it is well done
29	*haste me to know't:* tell me quickly
30	*meditation:* thoughts
31	*sweep:* attack quickly
	apt: willing to act
32	*duller:* reacting slowly
	fat weed: plenty of plants on river banks
33	*rots itself in ease:* decomposes quietly
	on Lethe wharf: before all is forgotten

Note, l. 33: Lethe [ˈliːθiː] is a river in the mythical Hades, the world of the dead, whose water caused people to forget.

34	*stir:* take action
35	*orchard:* garden
36	*a serpent stung:* a snake bit
37	*forgèd process:* false report
38	*rankly abused:* disgustingly deceived
40	*prophetic:* foretelling future events
42	*incestuous:* involving sex between close family members
	adulterate: adulterous; unfaithful
43	*traitorous:* treacherous, that cannot be trusted
	gifts: natural talents
45	*seduce sb.:* persuade sb. to have sex with you
46	*will:* sexual desire
	most seeming: only in appearance
	virtuous: having high moral standards
47	*falling off:* change for the worse
48	*dignity:* worth, value
50	*decline:* fall in a moral sense
51	*wretch:* miserable creature
54	*lewdness court:* lustfulness tries to please
55	*radiant:* showing great love or warmth
56	*sate:* satisfy with more than is needed
	celestial: heavenly
57	*prey:* feed
58	*scent:* smell

HAMLET: Murder?

GHOST: Murder most foul, as in the best it is;
But this most foul, strange, and unnatural.

HAMLET: Haste me to know't, that I, with wings as swift
30   As meditation or the thoughts of love,
May sweep to my revenge.

GHOST: I find thee apt;
And duller shouldst thou be than the fat weed
That rots itself in ease on Lethe wharf,
Wouldst thou not stir in this. Now, Hamlet, hear.
35   'Tis given out that, sleeping in my orchard,
A serpent stung me. So the whole ear of Denmark
Is by a forgèd process of my death
Rankly abused. But know, thou noble youth,
The serpent that did sting thy father's life
40   Now wears his crown.

HAMLET: O my prophetic soul!
My uncle?

GHOST: Ay, that incestuous, that adulterate beast,
With witchcraft of his wit, with traitorous gifts –
O wicked wit and gifts, that have the power
45   So to seduce! – won to his shameful lust
The will of my most seeming-virtuous queen.
O Hamlet, what a falling-off was there,
From me, whose love was of that dignity
That it went hand in hand even with the vow
50   I made to her in marriage, and to decline
Upon a wretch whose natural gifts were poor
To those of mine!
But virtue, as it never will be moved,
Though lewdness court it in a shape of heaven,
55   So lust, though to a radiant angel linked,
Will sate itself in a celestial bed
And prey on garbage.
But soft! Methinks I scent the morning air.

61 *secure:* unguarded; safe
62 *hebenon:* type of poison
   vial: small glass container
63 *porches:* entrances
64 *leperous distilment:* liquid causing leprosy (*Lepra*)
65 *enmity:* hostile opposition
66 *quicksilver:* mercury (*Quecksilber*)
67 *gates and alleys:* holes and passages
68 *vigour:* force
68–69 *posset and curd:* thicken and clot (the blood)
69 *eager:* acid
71 *tetter:* skin disease, rash
   barked about: covered the body with a crust similar to bark (*Baumrinde*)
72 *lazar-like:* like a person with leprosy
   vile and loathsome crust: evil, disgusting scab on the skin
75 *dispatched:* robbed, sent off
76 *in the blossoms:* at the height
77 *unhouseled:* without a Christian sacrament
   disappointed: not prepared by not having confessed his sins before death
   unaneled: not blessed by being touched with holy oil
78 *reckoning:* settling of debts
   account: final judgement on doomsday
79 *imperfections:* faults
81 *nature:* natural feeling
83 *luxury:* (sinful) lust
84 *howsomever:* in whatever manner
   pursuest: proceed, follow up
85 *taint:* corrupt
   contrive: lay schemes
86 *aught:* in any way
87 *thorns:* sharp pointed part on the stems of some plants
   lodge: live, reside
89 *glow-worm:* beetle emitting light from the belly
   matin: morning
90 *gins ... fire:* begins to lose its glow

Brief let me be. Sleeping within my orchard,
60 My custom always of the afternoon,
Upon my secure hour thy uncle stole,
With juice of cursèd hebenon in a vial,
And in the porches of my ears did pour
The leperous distilment; whose effect
65 Holds such an enmity with blood of man
That swift as quicksilver it courses through
The natural gates and alleys of the body,
And with a sudden vigour it doth posset
And curd, like eager droppings into milk,
70 The thin and wholesome blood. So did it mine;
And a most instant tetter barked about,
Most lazar-like, with vile and loathsome crust
All my smooth body.
Thus was I, sleeping, by a brother's hand
75 Of life, of crown, of queen, at once dispatched;
Cut off even in the blossoms of my sin,
Unhouseled, disappointed, unaneled,
No reckoning made, but sent to my account
With all my imperfections on my head.
80 **HAMLET:** O, horrible! O, horrible! Most horrible!
GHOST: If thou hast nature in thee, bear it not.
Let not the royal bed of Denmark be
A couch for luxury and damnèd incest.
But, howsomever thou pursuest this act,
85 Taint not thy mind, nor let thy soul contrive
Against thy mother aught. Leave her to heaven,
And to those thorns that in her bosom lodge
To prick and sting her. Fare thee well at once.
The glow-worm shows the matin to be near
90 And gins to pale his uneffectual fire.
Adieu, adieu, adieu! Remember me.

Exit.

92 *host of heaven:* army of angels
93 *couple:* include
94 *sinews:* bands that join a muscle to the bone (*Sehnen*)
      instant: immediately
97 *distracted:* unbalanced, distressed
98 *table:* notebook, writing tablet
99 *fond:* silly, foolish
      records: all that is written
100 *saws:* moral sayings, platitudes
       forms: conventional ideas
       pressures past: impressions of the past
104 *baser:* less important
105 *pernicious:* wicked, destructive
107 *meet:* fitting
115 *illo, ho, ho:* 'hello' shouted in a loud voice (a falconer's cry to his hawk)
118 *wonderful:* extraordinary

HAMLET: O all you host of heaven! O earth! What else?
And shall I couple hell? Hold, hold, my heart!
And you, my sinews, grow not instant old,
95   But bear me stiffly up. Remember thee?
Ay, thou poor ghost, while memory holds a seat
In this distracted globe. Remember thee?
Yea, from the table of my memory
I'll wipe away all trivial fond records,
100 All saws of books, all forms, all pressures past
That youth and observation copied there,
And thy commandment all alone shall live
Within the book and volume of my brain,
Unmixed with baser matter. Yes, by heaven!
105 O most pernicious woman!
O villain, villain, smiling, damnèd villain!
My tables! Meet it is I set it down
That one may smile, and smile, and be a villain;
At least I am sure it may be so in Denmark. *[Writes.]*
110 So, uncle, there you are. Now to my word:
It is 'Adieu, adieu! Remember me.'
I have sworn't.

HORATIO: *[Within]* My lord, my lord!

Enter HORATIO *and* MARCELLUS.

MARCELLUS: Lord Hamlet!
HORATIO: Heaven secure him!
HAMLET: So be it!
115 **MARCELLUS:** Illo, ho, ho, my lord!
HAMLET: Hillo, ho, ho, boy! Come, bird, come.
MARCELLUS: How is't, my noble lord?
HORATIO: What news, my lord?
MARCELLUS: O, wonderful!
HORATIO: Good my lord, tell it.
HAMLET: No, you will reveal it.

121 *once:* ever
125 *arrant knave:* absolute villain
128 *circumstance:* formality; details
134 *whirling:* confusing
137 *Saint Patrick:* patron saint of Ireland, believed to free sinners from purgatory
138 *touching:* regarding
139 *honest:* genuine
141 *o'ermaster't:* overcome it, get the better of it
143 *poor request:* small favour

120 **HORATIO:** Not I, my lord, by heaven!

MARCELLUS: Nor I, my lord.

HAMLET: How say you then? Would heart of man once think it?
    But you'll be secret?

MARCELLUS: ⎱
HORATIO: ⎰ Ay, by heaven, my lord.

HAMLET: There's ne'er a villain dwelling in all Denmark
125   But he's an arrant knave.

HORATIO: There needs no ghost, my lord, come from the grave
    To tell us this.

HAMLET: Why, right! You are in the right!
    And so, without more circumstance at all,
    I hold it fit that we shake hands and part;
130   You, as your business and desires shall point you,
    For every man hath business and desire,
    Such as it is; and for my own poor part,
    Look you, I'll go pray.

HORATIO: These are but wild and whirling words, my lord.

135 **HAMLET:** I am sorry they offend you, heartily;
    Yes, faith, heartily.

HORATIO: There's no offence, my lord.

HAMLET: Yes, by Saint Patrick, but there is, Horatio,
    And much offence too. Touching this vision here,
    It is an honest ghost, that let me tell you.
140   For your desire to know what is between us,
    O'ermaster't as you may. And now, good friends,
    As you are friends, scholars, and soldiers,
    Give me one poor request.

HORATIO: What is't, my lord? We will.

145 **HAMLET:** Never make known what you have seen tonight.

MARCELLUS: ⎱
HORATIO: ⎰ My lord, we will not.

HAMLET: Nay, but swear't.

HORATIO: In faith,
    My lord, not I.

Note, l. 149: The hilt of a sword looks like a cross, so swearing by a sword was common for Christians at the time.

152   *truepenny:* honest fellow
153   *cellerage:* cellar, space underground
154   *consent:* agree
158   *hic et ubique* (Latin): here and everywhere
      shift our ground: change places
164   *mole: Maulwurf*
165   *worthy pioneer:* excellent miner
      remove: move off
171   *so help you mercy:* as you are hoping for God's mercy
172   *some'er:* how ever
173   *perchance:* perhaps
      meet: suitable, acceptable
174   *antic disposition:* mad or bizarre behaviour
176   *encumbered:* folded in astonishment
177   *doubtful:* having different meanings

MARCELLUS: Nor I, my lord, in faith.

HAMLET: Upon my sword.

MARCELLUS: We have sworn, my lord, already.

150   **HAMLET:** Indeed, upon my sword, indeed.

GHOST *cries under the stage.*

GHOST: Swear.

HAMLET: Ha, ha, boy, sayest thou so? Art thou there, truepenny?
   Come on! You hear this fellow in the cellarage.
   Consent to swear.

HORATIO: Propose the oath, my lord.

155   **HAMLET:** Never to speak of this that you have seen.
   Swear by my sword.

GHOST: *[Beneath]* Swear.

HAMLET: Hic et ubique? Then we'll shift our ground.
   Come hither, gentlemen,

160   And lay your hands again upon my sword.
   Never to speak of this that you have heard:
   Swear by my sword.

GHOST: *[Beneath]* Swear by his sword.

HAMLET: Well said, old mole! Canst work i' th' earth so fast?

165   A worthy pioneer! Once more remove, good friends.

HORATIO: O day and night, but this is wondrous strange!

HAMLET: And therefore as a stranger give it welcome.
   There are more things in heaven and earth, Horatio,
   Than are dreamt of in your philosophy.

170   But come!
   Here, as before, never, so help you mercy,
   How strange or odd some'er I bear myself
   As I perchance hereafter shall think meet
   To put an antic disposition on,

175   That you, at such times seeing me, never shall,
   With arms encumbered thus, or this head-shake,
   Or by pronouncing of some doubtful phrase,

179 *list:* wished
180 *ambiguous giving out:* obscure declaration
        note: indicate
182 *grace and mercy:* divine salvation and forgiveness
185 *perturbèd:* impatient
186 *commend me:* entrust myself
188 *friending:* friendship
189 *lack:* be wanting
190 *still:* always
191 *out of joint:* in disorder
        cursèd spite: damned fortune

As 'Well, well, we know', or 'We could, and if we would',
Or 'If we list to speak', or 'There be, and if they might',
180 Or such ambiguous giving out, to note
That you know aught of me: this is not to do,
So grace and mercy at your most need help you,
Swear.
GHOST: *[Beneath]* Swear.

They swear.

185 **HAMLET:** Rest, rest, perturbèd spirit! So, gentlemen,
With all my love I do commend me to you;
And what so poor a man as Hamlet is
May do t' express his love and friending to you,
God willing, shall not lack. Let us go in together;
190 And still your fingers on your lips, I pray.
The time is out of joint. O cursèd spite
That ever I was born to set it right!
Nay, come, let's go together.

Exeunt.

Summary:

In his private rooms, Polonius sends his servant Reynaldo to take letters and money to Laertes in Paris. He wants him to find out from Laertes's friends if his son is behaving properly by dropping hints about Laertes's alleged bad behaviour, hoping to get information in this indirect way. Upset, Ophelia comes to tell her father that Hamlet came into her room in disordered clothes and acting strangely. Polonius concludes that the prince must have gone mad because of his love for Ophelia, and he goes to tell the king immediately.

Annotations:

  4   *make inquire:* find out
  7   *Danskers:* Danes
  8   *means* (pl): resources
       keep: live
10   *encompassment ... question:* general way of talking and asking questions
12   *touch:* come closer
13   *take you:* assume
19   *addicted:* given to a sinful life
20   *forgeries: falsche Anschuldigungen*
       rank: excessive
21   *take heed:* be careful
22   *wanton:* carefree, wild
       slips: imperfections
24   *gaming:* gambling

ACT II

Scene I

Elsinore. A room in the house of POLONIUS.

Enter POLONIUS *and* REYNALDO.

POLONIUS: Give him this money, and these notes, Reynaldo.
REYNALDO: I will, my lord.
POLONIUS: You shall do marvellous wisely, good Reynaldo,
    Before you visit him, to make inquire
5   Of his behaviour.
REYNALDO: My lord, I did intend it.
POLONIUS: Marry, well said, very well said. Look you, sir,
    Enquire me first what Danskers are in Paris,
    And how, and who, what means, and where they keep,
    What company, at what expense; and finding
10   By this encompassment and drift of question
    That they do know my son, come you more nearer
    Than your particular demands will touch it.
    Take you, as 'twere, some distant knowledge of him,
    As thus, 'I know his father and his friends,
15   And in part him.' Do you mark this, Reynaldo?
REYNALDO: Ay, very well, my lord.
POLONIUS: 'And in part him, but,' – you may say – 'not well.
    But if 't be he I mean, he's very wild,
    Addicted so and so' – and there put on him
20   What forgeries you please; marry, none so rank
    As may dishonour him – take heed of that,
    But, sir, such wanton, wild, and usual slips
    As are companions noted and most known
    To youth and liberty.
REYNALDO: As gaming, my lord?

26   *drabbing:* using prostitutes
28   *season it in the charge:* weaken the accusation
30   *incontinency:* excessive sexual misbehaviour
31   *breathe:* speak about
         quaintly: artfully (*geschickt*)
32   *taints of liberty:* faults resulting from too much freedom
34   *savageness:* wildness
         unreclaimèd blood: unrestrained passion
35   *of general assault:* that happens to everyone
37   *drift:* plan
38   *fetch of warrant:* acceptable trick
39   *sullies:* slanders
40   *as 'twere:* as if it were
         soiled: dirty
         i' th' working: while being made
42   *party in converse:* conversation partner
         sound (v): question
43   *having ever:* if he has ever
         prenominate: mentioned before
45   *closes ... consequence:* agrees with you like this
47   *addition:* form of address
50   *by the mass:* exclamation of slight annoyance

25 **POLONIUS:** Ay, or drinking, fencing, swearing, quarrelling,
   Drabbing. You may go so far.
REYNALDO: My lord, that would dishonour him.
POLONIUS: Faith, no, as you may season it in the charge.
   You must not put another scandal on him,
30   That he is open to incontinency,
   That's not my meaning. But breathe his faults so quaintly
   That they may seem the taints of liberty,
   The flash and outbreak of a fiery mind,
   A savageness in unreclaimèd blood,
35   Of general assault.
REYNALDO: But, my good lord –
POLONIUS: Wherefore should you do this?
REYNALDO: Ay, my lord,
   I would know that.
POLONIUS: Marry, sir, here's my drift,
   And I believe it is a fetch of warrant.
   You laying these slight sullies on my son,
40   As 'twere a thing a little soiled i' th' working,
   Mark you,
   Your party in converse, him you would sound,
   Having ever seen in the prenominate crimes
   The youth you breathe of guilty, be assured
45   He closes with you in this consequence:
   'Good sir', or so, or 'friend', or 'gentleman',
   According to the phrase or the addition
   Of man and country.
REYNALDO: Very good, my lord.
POLONIUS: And then, sir, does he this – he does – What was I
50   about to say? By the mass, I was about to say something! Where
   did I leave?
REYNALDO: At 'closes in the consequence', at 'friend, or so', and
   'gentleman'.
POLONIUS: At 'closes in the consequence' – ay, marry!
55   He closes thus: 'I know the gentleman.

58 *o'ertook in's rouse:* drunk
59 *falling out:* quarrelling
60–61 *house of sale; brothel:* house where people pay to have sex
61 *videlicet* (Latin): that is to say
62 *bait:* sth. put on a hook to catch fish
         carp: type of fish (*Karpfen*)
63 *of wisdom and of reach:* being widely experienced
64 *windlasses:* indirect advances
         assays of bias: indirect attempts
65 *by indirections:* by dishonest practice
         directions: straight courses, honest purposes
66 *lecture:* lesson
67 *have:* understand
70 *observe his inclination in yourself:* see what he is up to with your own eyes
72 *ply:* practice
74 *affrighted:* terrified
76 *closet* ['klɒzɪt]: private room
77 *doublet:* man's close-fitting jacket with buttons
         unbraced: unbuttoned
79 *ungartered:* without strings that tie the stocking to the leg
         down-gyvèd: fallen down
81 *piteous:* demanding pity
         purport: expression

I saw him yesterday', or 'th' other day',
Or then, or then, with such or such; 'and, as you say,
'There was a gaming'; 'there o'ertook in's rouse';
'There falling out at tennis'; or perchance,
60 'I saw him enter such a house of sale',
Videlicet, a brothel, or so forth. See you now,
Your bait of falsehood takes this carp of truth;
And thus do we of wisdom and of reach,
With windlasses and with assays of bias,
65 By indirections find directions out.
So, by my former lecture and advice,
Shall you my son. You have me, have you not?
REYNALDO: My lord, I have.
POLONIUS: God buy ye, fare ye well!
REYNALDO: Good my lord!
70 POLONIUS: Observe his inclination in yourself.
REYNALDO: I shall, my lord.
POLONIUS: And let him ply his music.
REYNALDO: Well, my lord.
POLONIUS: Farewell!

Exit REYNALDO.

Enter OPHELIA.

                    How now, Ophelia? What's the matter?
OPHELIA: O my lord, my lord, I have been so affrighted!
75 POLONIUS: With what, i' th' name of God?
OPHELIA: My lord, as I was sewing in my closet,
    Lord Hamlet, with his doublet all unbraced,
    No hat upon his head, his stockings fouled,
    Ungartered, and down-gyvèd to his ankle;
80 Pale as his shirt, his knees knocking each other,
    And with a look so piteous in purport

82 *loosèd out:* let out
89 *perusal:* careful examination
90 *as:* as if
92 *thrice:* three times
94 *bulk:* whole body
99 *bended:* turned, directed
101 *ecstasy:* madness
102 *property:* quality, nature
    foredoes: destroys
103 *undertakings:* actions
105 *afflict:* give pain
108 *repel:* reject
108–109 *denied his access to me:* refused to see him
110 *better heed:* more care
111 *quoted:* observed
    trifle: not treat you with respect
112 *wrack:* ruin your reputation, seduce
    beshrew: cursed be
113 *proper to:* typical of

As if he had been loosèd out of hell
To speak of horrors – he comes before me.
POLONIUS: Mad for thy love?
OPHELIA: My lord, I do not know,
85 But truly I do fear it.
POLONIUS: What said he?
OPHELIA: He took me by the wrist and held me hard;
Then goes he to the length of all his arm,
And, with his other hand thus o'er his brow,
He falls to such perusal of my face
90 As he would draw it. Long stayed he so;
At last, a little shaking of mine arm,
And thrice his head thus waving up and down,
He raised a sigh so piteous and profound
As it did seem to shatter all his bulk
95 And end his being. That done, he lets me go,
And with his head over his shoulder turned
He seemed to find his way without his eyes,
For out-a-doors he went without their helps
And to the last bended their light on me.
100 **POLONIUS:** Come, go with me. I will go seek the king.
This is the very ecstasy of love,
Whose violent property fordoes itself,
And leads the will to desperate undertakings
As oft as any passion under heaven
105 That does afflict our natures. I am sorry.
What, have you given him any hard words of late?
OPHELIA: No, my good lord; but, as you did command,
I did repel his letters and denied
His access to me.
POLONIUS: That hath made him mad.
110 I am sorry that with better heed and judgement
I had not quoted him. I feared he did but trifle
And meant to wrack thee; but beshrew my jealousy.
By heaven, it is as proper to our age

114 *cast beyond ourselves:* miscalculate
115 *the younger sort:* young people
116 *lack discretion:* not be thoughtful and kind
117 *close:* secret
   move: cause
118 *more ... love:* it causes more trouble when kept secret than if discussed
   openly

To cast beyond ourselves in our opinions
115 As it is common for the younger sort
To lack discretion. Come, go we to the king.
This must be known, which, being kept close, might move
More grief to hide than hate to utter love.
Come.

Exeunt.

Summary:

In the palace, Claudius and Gertrude have sent for Rosencrantz and Guildenstern, two of Hamlet's friends. They want them to spy on Hamlet in order to discover what is wrong with him. The ambassadors to Norway bring news that the Norwegian king has given his nephew Fortinbras money and ordered him to attack Poland. As the troops need to pass through Denmark, Claudius's permission is requested.

When the court has left, Hamlet comes in reading and Polonius tries to make sense of the answers Hamlet gives him, detecting some logic in them. After Rosencrantz and Guildenstern have joined Hamlet, he asks them directly if they were sent to sound him out, which they admit. They tell him of a group of travelling players on their way to the castle, which lifts Hamlet's melancholic mood considerably. Polonius returns with the players and Hamlet quotes a speech from a play about Priam's death, the legendary king of Troy, which is continued by the leading actor.

Alone, Hamlet berates himself for not having revenged his father yet for fear that the ghost is an evil spirit that lied to him. He resolves to find out whether this is true or not using a trick: He will have the players perform a simulation of his father's murder in the play The Murder of Gonzago, *for which he will write an extra speech.*

Observing Claudius' reaction, he will then be able to determine if the king is guilty or not.

Annotations:

2 *moreover that:* not only that
6 *sith nor:* since neither
7 *that it was:* what it was
10 *entreat:* ask earnestly
12 *neighboured to:* familiar with
 haviour: behaviour
13 *vouchsafe your rest:* consent to stay
15 *draw him on:* pull him along
16 *occasion:* opportunity
 glean: gather
17 *aught:* anything
 afflicts: distresses
18 *opened:* revealed
 remedy: help
21 *adheres:* is in agreement with
22 *gentry:* respectful behaviour
23 *expend:* spend
24 *supply and profit:* support and benefit
26 *fits:* is proper for
27 *sovereign:* royal
 of: over

Scene II

Elsinore. A room in the castle.

Flourish. Enter KING *and* QUEEN, ROSENCRANTZ *and* GUILDENSTERN, *with others.*

CLAUDIUS: Welcome, dear Rosencrantz and Guildenstern.
    Moreover that we much did long to see you,
    The need we have to use you did provoke
    Our hasty sending. Something have you heard
5   Of Hamlet's transformation – so I call it,
    Sith nor th' exterior nor the inward man
    Resembles that it was. What it should be,
    More than his father's death, that thus hath put him
    So much from th' understanding of himself,
10   I cannot dream of. I entreat you both,
    That, being of so young days brought up with him,
    And since so neighboured to his youth and haviour,
    That you vouchsafe your rest here in our court
    Some little time; so by your companies
15   To draw him on to pleasures, and to gather
    So much as from occasion you may glean,
    Whether aught to us unknown afflicts him thus
    That opened lies within our remedy.
GERTRUDE: Good gentlemen, he hath much talked of you,
20   And sure I am, two men there are not living
    To whom he more adheres. If it will please you
    To show us so much gentry and good will
    As to expend your time with us a while,
    For the supply and profit of our hope,
25   Your visitation shall receive such thanks
    As fits a king's remembrance.
ROSENCRANTZ: Both your Majesties
    Might, by the sovereign power you have of us,

28 *dread pleasures:* deeply respected will
29 *entreaty* (v): ask earnestly
30 *in the full bent:* totally
35 *beseech:* beg
38 *practices:* actions, behaviour
42 *still:* always
43 *liege* [liːʤ]: lord
44 *hold* (v): regard
47 *trail of policy:* cleverness
49 *lunacy:* madness
51 *admittance:* permission to enter
52 *fruit:* 1. final course of a meal, 2. the top news

Put your dread pleasures more into command
Than to entreaty.

GUILDENSTERN: But we both obey,
30   And here give up ourselves in the full bent
To lay our service freely at your feet,
To be commanded.

CLAUDIUS: Thanks, Rosencrantz and gentle Guildenstern.

GERTRUDE: Thanks, Guildenstern and gentle Rosencrantz.
35   And I beseech you instantly to visit
My too much changèd son. Go, some of you,
And bring these gentlemen where Hamlet is.

GUILDENSTERN: Heavens make our presence and our practices
Pleasant and helpful to him!

GERTRUDE: Ay, amen!

Exeunt ROSENCRANTZ *and* GUILDENSTERN, *with some* ATTEND-
ANTS.

Enter POLONIUS.

40   **POLONIUS:** Th' ambassadors from Norway, my good lord,
Are joyfully returned.

CLAUDIUS: Thou still hast been the father of good news.

POLONIUS: Have I, my lord? Assure you, my good liege,
I hold my duty, as I hold my soul,
45   Both to my God and to my gracious king;
And I do think – or else this brain of mine
Hunts not the trail of policy so sure
As it hath used to do – that I have found
The very cause of Hamlet's lunacy.

50   **CLAUDIUS:** O, speak of that! That do I long to hear.

POLONIUS: Give first admittance to th' ambassadors.
My news shall be the fruit to that great feast.

CLAUDIUS: Thyself do grace to them, and bring them in.

55   *head and source:* origin
     distemper: illness
56   *main:* main point
58   *sift:* examine in detail
59   *brother:* colleague
60   *desires:* good wishes
61   *upon our first:* as soon as we spoke about it
62   *levies:* army raised
64   *Polack:* King of Poland
65   *whereat grieved:* for which (he) felt sorry
66   *impotence:* weakness
67   *borne in hand:* deceived, misled
     arrests: orders to stop military activities
69   *rebuke:* warning
     in fine: in conclusion
71   *th' assay of arms:* the attempts to use military force
73   *crowns:* gold coins
74   *commission:* authority
77   *quiet pass:* safe passage
79   *allowance:* permission

Exit POLONIUS.

He tells me, my dear Gertrude, he hath found
55   The head and source of all your son's distemper.
GERTRUDE: I doubt it is no other but the main:
His father's death and our o'erhasty marriage.
CLAUDIUS: Well, we shall sift him.

Enter POLONIUS, VOLTEMAND *and* CORNELIUS.

Welcome, my good friends.
Say, Voltemand, what from our brother Norway?
60   **VOLTEMAND:** Most fair return of greetings and desires.
Upon our first, he sent out to suppress
His nephew's levies; which to him appeared
To be a preparation 'gainst the Polack;
But better looked into, he truly found
65   It was against your Highness; whereat grieved,
That so his sickness, age, and impotence
Was falsely borne in hand, sends out arrests
On Fortinbras; which he, in brief, obeys,
Receives rebuke from Norway, and in fine
70   Makes vow before his uncle never more
To give th' assay of arms against your Majesty.
Whereon old Norway, overcome with joy,
Gives him three thousand crowns in annual fee,
And his commission to employ those soldiers,
75   So levied as before, against the Polack;
With an entreaty, herein further shown,
That it might please you to give quiet pass
Through your dominions for this enterprise,
On such regards of safety and allowance
80   As therein are set down.

Gives a paper.

80   *it likes us well:* it pleases us greatly
81   *at our more considered time:* when we have more time for reflection
83   *well-took:* well done
86   *expostulate:* discuss
90   *brevity:* shortness, conciseness
         wit: intellectual capacity
91   *tediousness:* quality of not being interesting
         limbs [lɪmz]: legs and arms (*Extremitäten*)
         flourishes: decorations
95   *more matter, with less art:* come to the point, use less rhetoric
98   *figure:* figure of speech
102 *defect:* fault
103 *comes by:* has a
105 *perpend:* consider carefully
107 *mark:* take notice
108 *gather, and surmise:* think and draw your conclusions; come closer and take
         a look

CLAUDIUS: It likes us well;
And at our more considered time we'll read,
Answer, and think upon this business.
Meantime, we thank you for your well-took labour.
Go to your rest; at night we'll feast together.
85   Most welcome home!

Exeunt AMBASSADORS.

POLONIUS: This business is well ended.
My liege, and madam, to expostulate
What majesty should be, what duty is,
Why day is day, night is night, and time is time,
Were nothing but to waste night, day, and time.
90   Therefore, since brevity is the soul of wit,
And tediousness the limbs and outward flourishes,
I will be brief. Your noble son is mad.
Mad call I it, for, to define true madness,
What is't but to be nothing else but mad?
95   But let that go.
GERTRUDE: More matter, with less art.
POLONIUS: Madam, I swear I use no art at all.
That he is mad, 'tis true: 'tis true 'tis pity,
And pity 'tis 'tis true. A foolish figure!
But farewell it, for I will use no art.
100   Mad let us grant him then, and now remains
That we find out the cause of this effect,
Or rather say, the cause of this defect,
For this effect defective comes by cause.
Thus it remains, and the remainder thus.
105   Perpend.
I have a daughter – have while she is mine –
Who in her duty and obedience, mark,
Hath given me this. Now gather, and surmise.

109 *celestial:* heavenly
beautified: made beautiful
110 *ill; vile:* badly chosen
114 *stay:* wait
faithful: truthful
119 *I am ill:* I am untalented
numbers: verses
reckon: count
120 *groans:* long mournful sounds
121 *whilst this machine is to him:* as long as I live
124 *more above:* moreover
solicitings: pleadings
125 *fell out:* happened
129 *fain:* willingly
130 *on the wing:* developing
131 *perceived:* discovered
134 *played the desk:* hesitated and withheld the information
table-book: notebook
135 *given my heart a winking:* shut my eyes to ignore this love
mute and dumb: silent
136 *idle:* inactive, lazy
137 *round:* directly
138 *I did bespeak:* I said (to her)
139 *out of thy star:* beyond your reach

[Reads the letter.]

To the celestial, and my soul's idol, the most beautified Ophelia –
110   that's an ill phrase, a vile phrase, 'beautified' is a vile phrase.
But you shall hear. *These, in her excellent white bosom, these, et*
cetera.

GERTRUDE: Came this from Hamlet to her?

POLONIUS: Good madam, stay awhile. I will be faithful.

115   *Doubt thou the stars are fire,*
Doubt that the sun doth move,
Doubt truth to be a liar,
But never doubt I love.
O dear Ophelia, I am ill at these numbers, I have not art to reckon
120   *my groans; but that I love thee best, O most best, believe it. Adieu.*
Thine evermore, most dear lady, whilst this machine is to him,
Hamlet.
This, in obedience, hath my daughter shown me;
And more above, hath his solicitings,
125   As they fell out, by time, by means, and place,
All given to mine ear.

CLAUDIUS: But how hath she
Received his love?

POLONIUS: What do you think of me?

CLAUDIUS: As of a man faithful and honourable.

POLONIUS: I would fain prove so. But what might you think,
130   When I had seen this hot love on the wing
As I perceived it, I must tell you that,
Before my daughter told me, what might you,
Or my dear Majesty your queen here, think,
If I had played the desk or table-book,
135   Or given my heart a winking, mute and dumb,
Or looked upon this love with idle sight?
What might you think? No, I went round to work
And my young mistress thus I did bespeak:
'Lord Hamlet is a prince, out of thy star.

140 *prescripts:* instructions
141 *resort:* visits
142 *tokens:* gifts or solemn promises of love
143 *fruits:* results
144 *repulsed:* rejected
145 *fast:* abstinence from food
146 *watch:* sleeplessness
147 *lightness:* light-headedness
　　　 declension: gradual decline

Note, l. 154: Polonius's "Take this from this" may indicate that there is a stage
　　　 direction missing. Maybe he points from his head to his shoulders, meaning
　　　 "Chop off my head."

160 *loose:* set loose; allow to meet
161 *arras* ['ærəs]: large tapestry hanging on the wall
163 *thereon:* because of this
164 *assistant for a state:* political adviser
165 *carters:* wagon-drivers
166 *sadly:* seriously

140 This must not be.' And then I prescripts gave her,
That she should lock herself from his resort,
Admit no messengers, receive no tokens.
Which done, she took the fruits of my advice,
And he, repulsed – a short tale to make –
145 Fell into a sadness, then into a fast,
Thence to a watch, thence into a weakness,
Thence to a lightness, and, by this declension,
Into the madness wherein now he raves,
And all we mourn for.
CLAUDIUS: Do you think 'tis this?
150 GERTRUDE: It may be, very like.
POLONIUS: Hath there been such a time, I would fain know that,
That I have positively said ''Tis so',
When it proved otherwise?
CLAUDIUS: Not that I know.
POLONIUS: Take this from this, if this be otherwise.
155 If circumstances lead me, I will find
Where truth is hid, though it were hid indeed
Within the centre.
CLAUDIUS: How may we try it further?
POLONIUS: You know sometimes he walks for hours together
Here in the lobby.
GERTRUDE: So he does indeed.
160 POLONIUS: At such a time I'll loose my daughter to him.
Be you and I behind an arras then.
Mark the encounter: If he love her not,
And he not from his reason fallen thereon,
Let me be no assistant for a state,
165 But keep a farm and carters.
CLAUDIUS: We will try it.

Enter HAMLET, *reading on a book.*

GERTRUDE: But look where sadly the poor wretch comes reading.

168 *board:* greet and speak to
presently: at once
170 *God-a-mercy:* God have mercy on you, i.e. thank you
172 *fishmonger: Fischhändler*
179 *maggots:* small worms (*Maden*)
180 *kissing carrion:* piece of rotting flesh ready for the sun to shine upon
182 *conception:* process of receiving sth. or of becoming pregnant
183 *conceive:* become pregnant
184 *harping on:* coming back to (the topic of)
187 *extremity* [ɪkˈstreməti]: utmost suffering
193 *slanders:* false reports
rogue: rude person
195 *purging:* oozing, discharging (*ausscheiden*)
amber: resin (*Harz*)
196 *hams:* thighs or legs
197 *potently:* strongly
197–198 *hold it not honesty:* do not consider it proper behaviour

POLONIUS: Away, I do beseech you both, away.
I'll board him presently. O, give me leave.

Exeunt KING *and* QUEEN, *with* ATTENDANTS.

How does my good Lord Hamlet?
170 **HAMLET:** Well, God-a-mercy.
POLONIUS: Do you know me, my lord?
HAMLET: Excellent well. You are a fishmonger.
POLONIUS: Not I, my lord.
HAMLET: Then I would you were so honest a man.
175 **POLONIUS:** Honest, my lord?
HAMLET: Ay, sir. To be honest, as this world goes, is to be one man
picked out of ten thousand.
POLONIUS: That's very true, my lord.
HAMLET: For if the sun breed maggots in a dead dog, being a good
180 kissing carrion – Have you a daughter?
POLONIUS: I have, my lord.
HAMLET: Let her not walk i' th' sun. Conception is a blessing, but
not as your daughter may conceive. Friend, look to't.
POLONIUS: *[Aside]* How say you by that? Still harping on my
185 daughter. Yet he knew me not at first, he said I was a fishmon-
ger. He is far gone, far gone! And truly in my youth I suffered
much extremity for love, very near this. I'll speak to him again. –
What do you read, my lord?
HAMLET: Words, words, words.
190 **POLONIUS:** What is the matter, my lord?
HAMLET: Between who?
POLONIUS: I mean the matter that you read, my lord.
HAMLET: Slanders, sir, for the satirical rogue says here that old
men have grey beards, that their faces are wrinkled, their eyes
195 purging thick amber and plumtree gum, and that they have a
plentiful lack of wit, together with most weak hams. All which,
sir, though I most powerfully and potently believe, yet I hold it

203 *pregnant:* (here) meaningful; clever
205 *sanity:* mental health
       prosperously: successfully
206 *suddenly:* immediately
       contrive: devise, plan
210 *withal:* with
220 *indifferent:* neither good nor bad, average
222 *Fortune:* goddess of good luck
       the very button: at the very top
225–226 *in the middle of her favours:* averagely favoured by her; near her sexual
       organs

not honesty to have it thus set down. For you yourself, sir, shall grow old as I am if, like a crab, you could go backward.

200 **POLONIUS:** *[Aside]* Though this be madness, yet there is method in't. – Will you walk out of the air, my lord?

HAMLET: Into my grave?

POLONIUS: Indeed, that's out of the air. *[Aside]* How pregnant sometimes his replies are! A happiness that often madness

205 hits on, which reason and sanity could not so prosperously be delivered of. I will leave him and suddenly contrive the means of meeting between him and my daughter. – My honourable lord, I will most humbly take my leave of you.

HAMLET: You cannot, sir, take from me anything that I will more

210 willingly part withal; except my life, except my life, except my life.

Enter ROSENCRANTZ *and* GUILDENSTERN.

POLONIUS: Fare you well, my lord.

HAMLET: These tedious old fools!

POLONIUS: You go to seek the Lord Hamlet. There he is.

215 **ROSENCRANTZ:** *[To* POLONIUS*]* God save you, sir!

Exit POLONIUS.

GUILDENSTERN: My honoured lord!

ROSENCRANTZ: My most dear lord!

HAMLET: My excellent good friends! How dost thou, Guildenstern? Ah, Rosencrantz! Good lads, how do you both?

220 **ROSENCRANTZ:** As the indifferent children of the earth.

GUILDENSTERN: Happy in that we are not over-happy;
On Fortune's cap we are not the very button.

HAMLET: Nor the soles of her shoe?

ROSENCRANTZ: Neither, my lord.

225 **HAMLET:** Then you live about her waist, or in the middle of her favours?

227 *privates:* 1. low-ranking soldiers, 2. private parts, i.e. sexual organs
228 *secret parts:* genitals
229 *strumpet:* prostitute
232 *in particular:* in detail
238 *confines* [ˈkɒnfaɪnz], *wards:* prison cells
239 *dungeons:* underground prisons
245 *bounded:* shut up
249 *substance of the ambitious:* what fuels ambition
253 *bodies:* people without ambitions
254 *outstretched heroes:* powerful men
255 *fay:* faith
256 *wait upon:* accompany
257 *sort sb.:* class sb., put sb. in the same group as sb. else
259 *dreadfully attended:* awfully looked after
  in the beaten way of friendship: speaking among old friends
259–260 *what make you:* what do you do

GUILDENSTERN: Faith, her privates we.

HAMLET: In the secret parts of Fortune? O, most true! She is a strumpet. What news?

230 **ROSENCRANTZ:** None, my lord, but that the world's grown honest.

HAMLET: Then is doomsday near! But your news is not true. Let me question more in particular. What have you, my good friends, deserved at the hands of Fortune that she sends you to prison hither?

235 **GUILDENSTERN:** Prison, my lord?

HAMLET: Denmark's a prison.

ROSENCRANTZ: Then is the world one.

HAMLET: A goodly one, in which there are many confines, wards, and dungeons, Denmark being one o' th' worst.

240 **ROSENCRANTZ:** We think not so, my lord.

HAMLET: Why, then 'tis none to you; for there is nothing either good or bad but thinking makes it so. To me it is a prison.

ROSENCRANTZ: Why, then your ambition makes it one. 'Tis too narrow for your mind.

245 **HAMLET:** O God, I could be bounded in a nutshell and count myself a king of infinite space, were it not that I have bad dreams.

GUILDENSTERN: Which dreams indeed are ambition, for the very substance of the ambitious is merely the shadow of a dream.

250 **HAMLET:** A dream itself is but a shadow.

ROSENCRANTZ: Truly, and I hold ambition of so airy and light a quality that it is but a shadow's shadow.

HAMLET: Then are our beggars bodies, and our monarchs and outstretched heroes the beggars' shadows. Shall we to th'
255 court? For, by my fay, I cannot reason.

ROSENCRANTZ:
GUILDENSTERN: } We'll wait upon you.

HAMLET: No such matter! I will not sort you with the rest of my servants; for, to speak to you like an honest man, I am most dreadfully attended. But in the beaten way of friendship, what
260 make you at Elsinore?

263–264 *too dear a halfpenny:* not worth much
264 *inclining* (n): wish
268 *anything but to th' purpose:* anything irrelevant
270 *modesties:* sense of shame; decency
    not craft enough to colour: no skill to disguise
273 *conjure:* ask seriously
274 *the consonancy of our youth:* our friendship
275 *ever-preserved:* everlasting
    what more dear: what more important reasons
276 *proposer:* speaker; questioner
    charge: urge
    even: honest
279 *an eye of you:* an eye on you
282–283 *so ... discovery:* I'll say it first so that you will not have to tell me
283–284 *moult no feather:* remain undisturbed
285 *mirth:* happiness
    forgone: given up
    custom of exercises: usual activities
287 *sterile promontory: kahles Vorgebirge*
    canopy: roof-like cover
    brave: splendid
288 *firmament:* sky
289 *fretted:* decorated
290 *pestilent congregation:* stinking collection
    vapours: very small drops of liquid in the air
291-292 *infinite:* limitless
292 *faculties:* abilities
    express: well-made
293 *apprehension:* understanding
294 *paragon:* model
295 *quintessence:* fundamental nature; essence

ROSENCRANTZ: To visit you, my lord, no other occasion.

HAMLET: Beggar that I am, I am even poor in thanks, but I thank
you – and sure, dear friends, my thanks are too dear a halfpenny. Were you not sent for? Is it your own inclining? Is it a
265   free visitation? Come, deal justly with me. Come, come! Nay,
speak.

GUILDENSTERN: What should we say, my lord?

HAMLET: Why, anything but to th' purpose. You were sent for –
and there is a kind of confession in your looks, which your
270   modesties have not craft enough to colour. I know the good
king and queen have sent for you.

ROSENCRANTZ: To what end, my lord?

HAMLET: That you must teach me. But let me conjure you, by the
rights of our fellowship, by the consonancy of our youth, by the
275   obligation of our ever-preserved love, and by what more dear
a better proposer could charge you withal, be even and direct
with me, whether you were sent for or no.

ROSENCRANTZ: *[Aside to* GUILDENSTERN*]* What say you?

HAMLET: *[Aside]* Nay then, I have an eye of you. – If you love me,
280   hold not off.

GUILDENSTERN: My lord, we were sent for.

HAMLET: I will tell you why. So shall my anticipation prevent
your discovery, and your secrecy to the king and queen moult
no feather. I have of late, but wherefore I know not, lost all my
285   mirth, forgone all custom of exercises; and indeed, it goes so
heavily with my disposition that this goodly frame, the earth,
seems to me a sterile promontory; this most excellent canopy,
the air, look you, this brave o'erhanging firmament, this majestical roof fretted with golden fire – why, it appeareth no other
290   thing to me than a foul and pestilent congregation of vapours.
What a piece of work is a man! How noble in reason! How infinite in faculties, in form and moving how express and admirable, in action how like an angel, in apprehension how like a god!
The beauty of the world, the paragon of animals – and yet to
295   me, what is this quintessence of dust? Man delights not me –

302 *Lenten:* thin; poor (Lent = time of fasting)
303 *coted:* overtook
306 *tribute:* payment
306–307 *foil and target:* sword and shield
307 *humorous:* driven by a mood

Note, l. 307: The Elizabethan notion of the 'Four Humours' held that the human body contains four elements with corresponding liquids which should be evenly balanced for good health. It was believed that the elements were associated with a particular temperament and determined people's behaviour.

309 *tickle o' th' sere:* easily brought to laughter
310 *halt for't:* be interrupted
311 *wont to* [wɔʊnt]: used to
313 *how chances it:* how come
      residence: usual home
315 *inhibition:* ban on acting in their own theatre
316 *late innovation:* recent change in theatrical taste; ban on performing plays
317 *estimation:* reputation
320 *rusty:* not as good as before
321 *endeavour:* attempt
      wonted pace: usual quality

Note, ll. 322–326: In 1600, during the 'War of the Theatres', a company of boy actors had a lot of success with their satirical plays. They threatened the livelihood of the established adult theatre companies, who were then forced to tour the country to attract audiences.

322 *eyrie of children, little eyases:* noisy children, like little falcons
322–323 *cry out on the top of question:* dominate the debate
323 *tyrannically:* vehemently
324 *be-rattle:* noisily disturb
      common stages: public theatres
335 *rapiers:* small swords
326 *goose-quills:* goose feathers whose tips were used for writing
      dare scarce come thither: were afraid of being mocked
328 *escoted:* supported financially
      quality: acting profession
328–329 *no longer than they can sing:* until their voices break
330 *common:* adult
      like: likely

no, nor woman neither, though by your smiling you seem to say
so.

ROSENCRANTZ: My lord, there was no such stuff in my thoughts.

HAMLET: Why did you laugh then, when I said 'Man delights not
300   me'?

ROSENCRANTZ: To think, my lord, if you delight not in man, what
Lenten entertainment the players shall receive from you. We
coted them on the way, and hither are they coming to offer you
service.

305 **HAMLET:** He that plays the king shall be welcome, his majesty shall
have tribute of me; the adventurous knight shall use his foil and
target, the lover shall not sigh gratis, the humorous man shall
end his part in peace, the clown shall make those laugh whose
lungs are tickle o' th' sere, and the lady shall say her mind freely,
310   or the blank verse shall halt for't. What players are they?

ROSENCRANTZ: Even those you were wont to take such delight in,
the tragedians of the city.

HAMLET: How chances it they travel? Their residence, both in
reputation and profit, was better both ways.

315 **ROSENCRANTZ:** I think their inhibition comes by the means of the
late innovation.

HAMLET: Do they hold the same estimation they did when I was in
the city? Are they so followed?

ROSENCRANTZ: No indeed are they not.

320 **HAMLET:** How comes it? Do they grow rusty?

ROSENCRANTZ: Nay, their endeavour keeps in the wonted pace;
but there is, sir, an eyrie of children, little eyases, that cry out
on the top of question and are most tyrannically clapped for't.
These are now the fashion, and so be-rattle the common stages
325   – so they call them – that many wearing rapiers are afraid of
goose-quills and dare scarce come thither.

HAMLET: What, are they children? Who maintains 'em? How
are they escoted? Will they pursue the quality no longer than
they can sing? Will they not say afterwards, if they should
330   grow themselves to common players – as it is most like, if their

331 *means:* financial resources
332 *succession:* future profession
334 *tar:* provoke
336 *went to cuffs:* fought
338 *throwing about of brains:* clashing of opinions
339 *carry it away:* get away with it
333 *load:* weight

Note, l. 340: In Greek mythology, Hercules temporarily relieved Atlas, who carried the heavens on his shoulder, from his load.

343 *make mouths:* ridicule
344 *ducats:* gold coins many European countries used
   picture in little: miniature portrait
349 *th' appurtenance of:* what accompanies
   fashion: custom
350 *comply with:* give a proper welcome
   garb: way, manner
   lest my extent: for fear that my offering
355 *north-north-west:* only slightly
356 *hawk:* type of bird of prey (*Habicht*)
   handsaw: heron (*Reiher*)

means are no better, their writers do them wrong to make them
exclaim against their own succession?

ROSENCRANTZ: Faith, there has been much to do on both sides,
and the nation holds it no sin to tar them to controversy. There

335   was, for a while, no money bid for argument unless the poet
and the player went to cuffs in the question.

HAMLET: Is't possible?

GUILDENSTERN: O, there has been much throwing about of brains.

HAMLET: Do the boys carry it away?

340   **ROSENCRANTZ:** Ay, that they do, my lord, Hercules and his load
too.

HAMLET: It is not very strange, for my uncle is King of Denmark,
and those that would make mouths at him while my father
lived give twenty, forty, fifty, a hundred ducats apiece for his

345   picture in little. 'Sblood, there is something in this more than
natural, if philosophy could find it out.

Flourish for the PLAYERS.

GUILDENSTERN: There are the players.

HAMLET: Gentlemen, you are welcome to Elsinore. Your hands,
come! Th' appurtenance of welcome is fashion and ceremony.

350   Let me comply with you in this garb, lest my extent to the players, which I tell you must show fairly outwards, should more
appear like entertainment than yours. You are welcome. But my
uncle-father and aunt-mother are deceived.

GUILDENSTERN: In what, my dear lord?

355   **HAMLET:** I am but mad north-north-west. When the wind is
southerly, I know a hawk from a handsaw.

Enter POLONIUS.

POLONIUS: Well be with you, gentlemen!

358 *hark:* listen
360 *swaddling clouts:* baby clothes
361 *happily:* perhaps
363 *prophesy* (v): foretell future events
369 *buzz:* exclamation rejecting nonsense
373 *pastoral:* play representing life in the country
374–375 *scene individable:* not separated in single parts, following the unity of time, place and action
375 *poem unlimited:* not observing the rules of dramatic unity
375–376 *Seneca, Plautus:* Roman dramatists known for tragedies and comedies
376 *the law of writ and the liberty:* the rules of writing (e.g. regarding the unity of time and place) that a dramatist may or may not follow
378 *Jephtha:* military leader who sacrificed his daughter to God
381–382 *'One … well':* quote from a popular ballad of the time
386 *passing:* extremely
390 *by lot: durch Losentscheid*
wot: knows

HAMLET: Hark you, Guildenstern – and you too – at each ear
a hearer! That great baby you see there is not yet out of his
360   swaddling clouts.

ROSENCRANTZ: Happily he's the second time come to them, for
they say an old man is twice a child.

HAMLET: I will prophesy: he comes to tell me of the players, mark
it. – You say right, sir; a Monday morning; 'twas so indeed.

365 **POLONIUS:** My lord, I have news to tell you.

HAMLET: My lord, I have news to tell you. When Roscius was an
actor in Rome –

POLONIUS: The actors are come hither, my lord.

HAMLET: Buzz, buzz!

370 **POLONIUS:** Upon my honour.

HAMLET: Then came each actor on his ass –

POLONIUS: The best actors in the world, either for tragedy,
comedy, history, pastoral, pastoral-comical, historical-pastoral,
tragical-historical, tragical-comical-historical-pastoral, scene
375   individable, or poem unlimited. Seneca cannot be too heavy,
nor Plautus too light. For the law of writ and the liberty, these
are the only men.

HAMLET: O Jephtha, judge of Israel, what a treasure hadst thou!

POLONIUS: What treasure had he, my lord?

380 **HAMLET:** Why,

>   *One fair daughter, and no more,*
>   *The which he lovèd passing well.*

POLONIUS: *[Aside]* Still on my daughter.

HAMLET: Am I not i' th' right, old Jephtha?

385 **POLONIUS:** If you call me Jephtha, my lord, I have a daughter that I
love passing well.

HAMLET: Nay, that follows not.

POLONIUS: What follows then, my lord?

HAMLET: Why,

390 >   *As by lot, God wot,*
and then, you know –
>   *It came to pass, as most like it was.*

393 *row:* verse, line
    pious chanson: religious song
394 *abridgement:* interruption
397 *valanced:* bearded
    beard (v): confront
398 *by'r lady:* by the Virgin Mary
    ladyship: spoken to a male teenage actor who plays women's roles
399 *nearer to heaven:* taller
400 *altitude of a chopine:* height of a high-heeled shoe
400–401 *uncurrent gold:* cracked coins not worth the value
402 *we'll e'en to't:* we shall go directly to it
402–403 *fly at anything we see:* have a go at anything
403 *straight:* right away
404 *quality:* skill
407 *not above once:* not more than once
408 *the million:* a large number of people
    caviary to the general: expensive food (caviar) wasted on the general public
410 *cried in the top of mine:* was superior to mine
    digested: arranged
411 *cunning:* skill
412 *sallets:* vulgar phrases
413 *savoury:* more pleasing
414 *indict* [ɪnˈdaɪt]: accuse, prove guilty
    affectation: artificial showing off
415 *wholesome:* reasonable
415–416 *more handsome than fine:* more graceful than showy
416 *Aeneas:* prominent Trojan leader
417 *Dido* [ˈdaɪdəʊ]: Queen of Carthage
    Priam: King of Troy
420 *rugged:* rough
    Pyrrhus: one of the Trojan warriors hidden in the wooden horse
    Hyrcanian beast: mythical tiger known for its wildness
422 *sable arms:* black armour
424 *couchèd:* hidden
    ominous: fatal

The first row of the pious chanson will show you more, for look where my abridgment comes.

Enter the PLAYERS.

395 You are welcome, masters, welcome, all. I am glad to see thee well. Welcome, good friends. O, my old friend! Why, thy face is valanced since I saw thee last. Com'st thou to beard me in Denmark? What, my young lady and mistress? By'r lady, your ladyship is nearer to heaven than when I saw you last by the
400 altitude of a chopine. Pray God your voice, like a piece of uncurrent gold, be not cracked within the ring. Masters, you are all welcome. We'll e'en to't like French falconers, fly at anything we see. We'll have a speech straight. Come, give us a taste of your quality. Come, a passionate speech.
405 **FIRST PLAYER:** What speech, my good lord?

HAMLET: I heard thee speak me a speech once, but it was never acted; or if it was, not above once, for the play, I remember, pleased not the million, 'twas caviary to the general. But it was, as I received it, and others, whose judgements in such
410 matters cried in the top of mine, an excellent play, well digested in the scenes, set down with as much modesty as cunning. I remember one said there were no sallets in the lines to make the matter savoury, nor no matter in the phrase that might indict the author of affectation, but called it an honest method,
415 as wholesome as sweet, and by very much more handsome than fine. One speech in't I chiefly loved, 'twas Aeneas' tale to Dido, and thereabout of it especially where he speaks of Priam's slaughter. If it live in your memory, begin at this line, let me see, let me see:
420 *The rugged Pyrrhus, like th' Hyrcanian beast –*
'Tis not so, it begins with Pyrrhus –
The rugged Pyrrhus, he whose sable arms,
Black as his purpose, did the night resemble
When he lay couchèd in the ominous horse,

425 *dread:* inspiring fear
complexion: skin
426 *heraldry more dismal:* more gloomy markings, like insignia
427 *total gules:* covered in blood
tricked: decorated
429 *baked and impasted:* dried and hardened into a crust
parching: heated; burning
430 *tyrannous:* harsh
431 *wrath* [rɒθ]: extreme rage
432 *o'ersizèd with coagulated gore:* with a thick covering of blood
433 *carbuncles:* precious stones glowing red
434 *grandsire:* grandfather
435 *proceed:* continue
437 *discretion:* taste; judgement
438 *anon:* shortly after
439 *antique:* old
440 *rebellious:* disobedient
441 *repugnant to command:* resistant to orders
443 *with the whiff and wind:* i.e. only hitting air
     fell: cruel
444 *unnervèd:* weakened
senseless Ilium: unfeeling, unreasonable (King of) Troy
446 *stoops to his base:* falls to the ground
hideous: ghastly
447 *takes prisoner Pyrrhus' ear:* confuses and stops him in action
for lo: (exclamation) look
448 *declining:* moving downwards
milky: white-haired
449 *reverend:* highly respected
450 *painted:* like in a painting, i.e. motionless
451 *neutral to his will and matter:* unable to react
453 *against:* in
454 *rack:* clouds
455 *orb:* earth
456 *hush:* silent
457 *rend the region:* split the sky
458 *rousèd:* woken up from sleep
459 *Cyclops:* in Greek mythology, giant one-eyed creatures working as
blacksmiths

425   *Hath now this dread and black complexion smeared*
     With heraldry more dismal. Head to foot
     Now is he total gules, horridly tricked
     With blood of fathers, mothers, daughters, sons,
     Baked and impasted with the parching streets,
430   *That lend a tyrannous and a damnèd light*
     To their lord's murder. Roasted in wrath and fire,
     And thus o'ersizèd with coagulate gore,
     With eyes like carbuncles, the hellish Pyrrhus
     Old grandsire Priam seeks –

435 So, proceed you.

POLONIUS: 'Fore God, my lord, well spoken, with good accent and good discretion.

FIRST PLAYER: *Anon he finds him,*
     Striking too short at Greeks. His antique sword,
440   *Rebellious to his arm, lies where it falls,*
     Repugnant to command. Unequal matched,
     Pyrrhus at Priam drives, in rage strikes wide,
     But with the whiff and wind of his fell sword
     Th' unnervèd father falls. Then senseless Ilium,
445   *Seeming to feel this blow, with flaming top*
     Stoops to his base, and with a hideous crash
     Takes prisoner Pyrrhus' ear. For lo, his sword,
     Which was declining on the milky head
     Of reverend Priam, seemed i' th' air to stick.
450   *So, as a painted tyrant, Pyrrhus stood,*
     And, like a neutral to his will and matter,
     Did nothing.
     But, as we often see against some storm,
     A silence in the heavens, the rack stand still,
455   *The bold winds speechless, and the orb below*
     As hush as death, anon the dreadful thunder
     Doth rend the region; so, after Pyrrhus' pause,
     A rousèd vengeance sets him new a-work;
     And never did the Cyclops' hammers fall

460 *Mars:* god of war
forged for proof eterne: made to resist enemies forever
461 *remorse:* pangs of conscience; pity
463 *strumpet* (adj): untrustworthy
464 *synod:* assembly
465 *spokes and fellies:* wooden bars and rim of a wheel

Note, ll. 463–467: The Elizabethan concept of the Wheel of Fortune symbolises the idea that fortune or fate rule people's lives who are placed on a wheel moving either upward for success or downward for failure or death.

466 *bowl:* push
nave: hub, centre of a wheel (*Nabe*)
467 *fiends:* devils
469 *it shall to the barber's:* it will be cut
470 *jig:* comic scene including singing and dancing
bawdry: derber, anzüglicher Humor
471 *Hecuba:* King Priam's wife, Queen of Troy
472 *mobled:* (invented word) covered with a piece of cloth
476 *bisson rheum:* blinding tears
clout: piece of cloth
477 *late:* earlier
diadem: crown
478 *lank and all o'er-teemèd:* thin and worn out by having many children
loins: Lenden
480 *with tongue in venom steeped:* cursing loudly (venom = poison)
481 *state:* rule
pronounced: spoken
483 *make malicious sport:* kill brutally
484 *mincing:* hacking to pieces
limbs [lɪmz]: legs and arms (*Extremitäten*)
485 *burst of clamour:* sudden outcry
487 *milch* (adj): milky, cloudy
488 *passion:* pity
489 *turned his colour:* changed his natural skin colour
492 *well bestowed:* looked after properly; lodged
493 *used:* treated
493–494 *they ... chronicles:* they summarize the events of our time

460 *On Mars's armour, forged for proof eterne,*
With less remorse than Pyrrhus' bleeding sword
Now falls on Priam.
Out, out, thou strumpet Fortune! All you gods,
In general synod take away her power,
465 *Break all the spokes and fellies from her wheel,*
And bowl the round nave down the hill of heaven
As low as to the fiends!

POLONIUS: This is too long.

HAMLET: It shall to the barber's, with your beard. Prithee say on.
470 He's for a jig or a tale of bawdry, or he sleeps. Say on, come to
Hecuba.

FIRST PLAYER: *But who, O who, had seen the mobled queen –*

HAMLET: 'The mobled queen'?

POLONIUS: That's good! 'Mobled queen' is good.

475 **FIRST PLAYER:** *Run barefoot up and down, threat'ning the flames*
With bisson rheum; a clout upon that head
Where late the diadem stood, and for a robe,
About her lank and all o'erteemèd loins,
A blanket, in the alarm of fear caught up –
480 *Who this had seen, with tongue in venom steeped*
'Gainst Fortune's state would treason have pronounced.
But if the gods themselves did see her then,
When she saw Pyrrhus make malicious sport
In mincing with his sword her husband's limbs,
485 *The instant burst of clamour that she made*
Unless things mortal move them not at all,
Would have made milch the burning eyes of heaven
And passion in the gods.

POLONIUS: Look, where he has not turned his colour, and has
490 tears in's eyes. Prithee no more.

HAMLET: 'Tis well. I'll have thee speak out the rest of this soon. –
Good my lord, will you see the players well bestowed? Do you
hear? Let them be well used, for they are the abstract and brief

495 *epitaph:* inscription on a gravestone
    ill: bad
496 *to their desert:* to what they deserve
497 *God's bodkin:* (exclamation) by God's body
    after: according to
498 *'scape:* escape; be saved from
    whipping: punishment by hitting with a leather strap (common for
    'vagabonds', i.e. homeless people travelling from place to place)
500 *bounty:* generosity
506 *for a need study:* if necessary memorize
508 *insert:* put in
514 *God buy:* goodbye
515 *rogue and peasant* (attr): worthless and low-minded
518 *conceit:* imagination

chronicles of the time. After your death you were better have a
495   bad epitaph than their ill report while you live.

POLONIUS: My lord, I will use them according to their desert.

HAMLET: God's bodkin, man, much better. Use every man after his
desert, and who should 'scape whipping? Use them after your
own honour and dignity. The less they deserve, the more merit
500   is in your bounty. Take them in.

POLONIUS: Come, sirs.

HAMLET: Follow him, friends. We'll hear a play tomorrow.

Exeunt POLONIUS *and* PLAYERS *except the* FIRST PLAYER.

Dost thou hear me, old friend? Can you play 'The Murder of
Gonzago'?
505 **FIRST PLAYER:** Ay, my lord.

HAMLET: We'll ha't tomorrow night. You could for a need study a
speech of some dozen or sixteen lines, which I would set down
and insert in't, could you not?

FIRST PLAYER: Ay, my lord.
510 **HAMLET:** Very well. Follow that lord, and look you mock him not.

Exit FIRST PLAYER.

My good friends, I'll leave you till night. You are welcome to
Elsinore.

ROSENCRANTZ: Good my lord.

HAMLET: Ay, so, God buy to you.

Exeunt ROSENCRANTZ *and* GUILDENSTERN.

                Now I am alone.
515   O what a rogue and peasant slave am I!
Is it not monstrous that this player here,
But in a fiction, in a dream of passion,
Could force his soul so to his own conceit

519 *his visage wanned:* his face became pale
520 *distraction:* despair
in's aspect: in his look
521–522 *his whole function suiting with forms:* his performance matching
526 *motive:* provocation
cue for passion: reason for suffering (cue = signal for an actor to say, show or do something)
528 *cleave:* split, cut in two
the general ear: the audience's ears
529 *appal the free:* shock the innocent
530 *confound the ignorant:* confuse those who do not know about it
amaze: terrify
531 *faculties:* functioning
532 *a dull and muddy-mettled rascal:* a stupid and cowardly good-for-nothing
peak: be forced to wait and suffer for a long time
533 *John-a-dreams:* day-dreamer
unpregnant: lethargic, not motivated to act
535 *property:* kingdom
536 *defeat:* destructive attack
537 *pate:* top of the head
538 *plucks:* pulls
539 *tweaks:* pinches
gives me the lie i' th' throat: calls me a liar
541 *'swounds:* (exclamation) by God's wounds
542 *pigeon-livered:* cowardly
gall: courage
543 *oppression:* distress
ere: before
544 *fatted:* fed; made fat
kite: type of bird of prey (*Milan*)
545 *offal:* inside parts of an animal
bawdy: derb, obszön
546 *remorseless:* pitiless
lecherous: lustful
kindless: unnatural, degenerate
548 *brave:* fine
550 *prompted:* motivated
552 *fall a-cursing:* begin to curse
drab: prostitute
553 *scullion:* kitchen servant

That, from her working, all his visage wanned,
520   Tears in his eyes, distraction in's aspect,
A broken voice, and his whole function suiting
With forms to his conceit? And all for nothing?
For Hecuba!
What's Hecuba to him, or he to Hecuba,
525   That he should weep for her? What would he do,
Had he the motive and the cue for passion
That I have? He would drown the stage with tears
And cleave the general ear with horrid speech,
Make mad the guilty and appal the free,
530   Confound the ignorant, and amaze indeed
The very faculties of eyes and ears. Yet I,
A dull and muddy-mettled rascal, peak
Like John-a-dreams, unpregnant of my cause,
And can say nothing! No, not for a king,
535   Upon whose property and most dear life
A damned defeat was made. Am I a coward?
Who calls me villain? Breaks my pate across?
Plucks off my beard and blows it in my face?
Tweaks me by th' nose, gives me the lie i' th' throat
540   As deep as to the lungs? Who does me this?
Ha, 'swounds, I should take it, for it cannot be
But I am pigeon-livered and lack gall
To make oppression bitter, or ere this
I should have fatted all the region kites
545   With this slave's offal. Bloody, bawdy villain!
Remorseless, treacherous, lecherous, kindless villain!
O, vengeance!
Why, what an ass am I! This is most brave,
That I, the son of a dear father murderèd,
550   Prompted to my revenge by heaven and hell,
Must like a whore unpack my heart with words
And fall a-cursing like a very drab,
A scullion!

554 *foh!:* (exclamation) get going!
556 *cunning:* clever realization
557 *presently:* at once
558 *proclaimed their malefactions:* confessed their crimes
560 *organ:* voice
563 *tent him to the quick: reize ihn bis aufs Blut*
    blench: flinch
568 *potent:* effective
569 *abuses:* deceives
    grounds: reasons
570 *relative:* relevant, substantial

Fie upon't! Foh! About, my brain! Hum, I have heard
555   That guilty creatures, sitting at a play,
Have by the very cunning of the scene
Been struck so to the soul that presently
They have proclaimed their malefactions;
For murder, though it have no tongue, will speak
560   With most miraculous organ. I'll have these players
Play something like the murder of my father
Before mine uncle. I'll observe his looks,
I'll tent him to the quick. If he but blench,
I know my course. The spirit that I have seen
565   May be a devil – and the devil hath power
T' assume a pleasing shape. Yea, and perhaps
Out of my weakness and my melancholy,
As he is very potent with such spirits,
Abuses me to damn me. I'll have grounds
570   More relative than this. The play's the thing
Wherein I'll catch the conscience of the king.

Exit.

Summary:

Rosencrantz and Guildenstern report to the royal couple that they could not find an explanation for Hamlet's unusual behaviour. Having sent for Hamlet and hiding behind a tapestry on the wall, Claudius and Polonius plan to observe Ophelia's 'accidental' encounter with the prince to find out if he is really mad because she rejected him. Hamlet, thinking himself to be alone, wonders if he should kill himself and reflects on death and the afterlife. When he notices Ophelia, he approaches her. She tries to return the gifts he sent her, which enrages him. He severely insults Ophelia, accuses her of dishonesty, rails against marriage and tells her to go to a nunnery, which upsets her greatly. Unlike Polonius, Claudius thinks there are reasons other than lovesickness for Hamlet's actions and decides to send him to England, hoping the change will improve his mental condition. Polonius's idea is that Gertrude should talk to her son and find out what troubles him. He offers to spy on this meeting as well.

Annotations:

1   *drift of conference:* indirect questions; roundabout talk
3   *grating:* spoiling
5   *distracted:* confused
7   *forward to be sounded:* willing to be questioned
8   *crafty:* cunning; sly
10   *true state:* real mental condition
12   *disposition:* mood, behaviour
13   *niggard of question:* unwilling to talk
     demands: questions
14   *assay:* tempt, persuade
16   *so fell out:* happened
17   *o'erraught:* overtook

ACT III

Scene I

Elsinore. A room in the castle.

Enter KING, QUEEN, POLONIUS, OPHELIA, ROSENCRANTZ, GUILDEN-
STERN, *and* LORDS.

CLAUDIUS: And can you by no drift of conference
    Get from him why he puts on this confusion,
    Grating so harshly all his days of quiet
    With turbulent and dangerous lunacy?
5 ROSENCRANTZ: He does confess he feels himself distracted,
    But from what cause he will by no means speak.
GUILDENSTERN: Nor do we find him forward to be sounded,
    But with a crafty madness keeps aloof
    When we would bring him on to some confession
10   Of his true state.
GERTRUDE: Did he receive you well?
ROSENCRANTZ: Most like a gentleman.
GUILDENSTERN: But with much forcing of his disposition.
ROSENCRANTZ: Niggard of question, but of our demands
    Most free in his reply.
GERTRUDE: Did you assay him
15   To any pastime?
ROSENCRANTZ: Madam, it so fell out that certain players
    We o'erraught on the way. Of these we told him,
    And there did seem in him a kind of joy
    To hear of it. They are about the court,
20   And, as I think, they have already order
    This night to play before him.

22 *beseeched:* begged
    entreat: ask earnestly
25 *inclined:* disposed
26 *a further edge:* more encouragement
27 *drive his purpose on:* support his plans
29 *closely:* secretly
31 *affront:* meet, face
32 *lawful espials:* legitimate spies
33 *bestow:* hide
36 *affliction:* suffering
39 *good beauties:* virtuous qualities
40 *wildness:* madness
41 *wonted way* [ˈwəʊntɪd]: usual behaviour
42 *honours:* credit
43 *Gracious:* your Grace
45 *exercise:* practice
45–46 *colour your loneliness:* illustrate that you are alone

POLONIUS: 'Tis most true;
    And he beseeched me to entreat your Majesties
    To hear and see the matter.
CLAUDIUS: With all my heart, and it doth much content me
25   To hear him so inclined.
    Good gentlemen, give him a further edge
    And drive his purpose on to these delights.
ROSENCRANTZ: We shall, my lord.

Exeunt ROSENCRANTZ *and* GUILDENSTERN.

CLAUDIUS: Sweet Gertrude, leave us too;
    For we have closely sent for Hamlet hither,
30   That he, as 'twere by accident, may here
    Affront Ophelia.
    Her father and myself, lawful espials,
    Will so bestow ourselves that, seeing unseen,
    We may of their encounter frankly judge
35   And gather by him, as he is behaved,
    If 't be th' affliction of his love, or no,
    That thus he suffers for.
GERTRUDE: I shall obey you;
    And for your part, Ophelia, I do wish
    That your good beauties be the happy cause
40   Of Hamlet's wildness. So shall I hope your virtues
    Will bring him to his wonted way again,
    To both your honours.
OPHELIA: Madam, I wish it may.

Exit QUEEN.

POLONIUS: Ophelia, walk you here. – Gracious, so please you,
    We will bestow ourselves. – *[To* OPHELIA*]* Read on this book,
45   That show of such an exercise may colour
    Your loneliness. – We are oft to blame in this:

47   *devotion's visage:* show of religiousness
48   *pious:* showing respect for religion
         sugar o'er: sweeten
50   *how smart a lash:* how painful a hit
51   *harlot:* prostitute
         plastering art: make-up
53   *painted:* deceitful
58   *slings and arrows:* catapults and pointed thin sticks shot from a bow
         outrageous: scandalous
62   *natural shocks:* pain or blows that nature has in store
63   *is heir to:* inherits from its ancestors
         consummation: accomplishment; ending
65   *perchance:* perhaps
         rub: problem, obstacle
66   *shuffled off this mortal coil:* got rid of our body, i.e. died
68   *give:* make
         respect: consideration
69   *calamity:* great misfortune
         of so long life: continue for so long
70   *whips and scorns:* strokes and insults
71   *contumely:* insulting behaviour
72   *disprized:* undervalued
         the law's delay: delaying tactics of judges
73   *the insolence of office:* impertinence of those holding office
         spurns (n): kicks
74   *that ... takes:* that people of good qualities suffer from those who are
         unworthy
75   *quietus:* death

'Tis too much proved, that with devotion's visage
And pious action we do sugar o'er
The devil himself.
CLAUDIUS: *[Aside]*   O, 'tis too true!
50 How smart a lash that speech doth give my conscience!
The harlot's cheek, beautied with plastering art,
Is not more ugly to the thing that helps it
Than is my deed to my most painted word.
O heavy burden!
55 **POLONIUS:** I hear him coming. Let's withdraw, my lord.

Exeunt KING *and* POLONIUS.

Enter HAMLET.

HAMLET: To be, or not to be, that is the question:
Whether 'tis nobler in the mind to suffer
The slings and arrows of outrageous fortune,
Or to take arms against a sea of troubles,
60 And by opposing end them. To die, to sleep –
No more; and by a sleep to say we end
The heartache, and the thousand natural shocks
That flesh is heir to – 'tis a consummation
Devoutly to be wished. To die, to sleep –
65 To sleep, perchance to dream. Ay, there's the rub!
For in that sleep of death what dreams may come,
When we have shuffled off this mortal coil,
Must give us pause. There's the respect
That makes calamity of so long life,
70 For who would bear the whips and scorns of time,
Th' oppressor's wrong, the proud man's contumely,
The pangs of disprized love, the law's delay,
The insolence of office, and the spurns
That patient merit of th' unworthy takes,
75 When he himself might his quietus make

76 *bare bodkin:* short dagger
    fardels: burdens
79 *bourn:* border
85 *sicklied o'er with the pale cast of thought:* is spoiled by thinking too much

Note, ll. 84–85: The 'native hue of resolution', i.e. the colour that signifies
    determination to act, is red – the colour of blood. Too much thinking turns
    healthy red into an unhealthy pale (*blass*) colour.

86 *pitch and moment:* importance
87 *currents turn awry:* direction is lost
89 *nymph:* chaste goddess of the waters, i.e. Ophelia
    orisons: prayers
91 *for this many a day:* during the past few days
93 *remembrances:* gifts, keepsakes
96 *aught:* anything
101 *wax* (v): grow
103 *honest:* truthful; chaste (i.e. a virgin)
105 *fair:* beautiful; pure
107 *honesty:* goodness; chastity (the state of not having sex)
107–108 *your honesty ... beauty:* your goodness and chastity should have
    nothing to do with your beauty

With a bare bodkin? Who would these fardels bear,
To grunt and sweat under a weary life,
But that the dread of something after death,
The undiscovered country, from whose bourn
80   No traveller returns, puzzles the will,
And makes us rather bear those ills we have
Than fly to others that we know not of?
Thus conscience does make cowards of us all,
And thus the native hue of resolution
85   Is sicklied o'er with the pale cast of thought,
And enterprises of great pitch and moment
With this regard their currents turn awry
And lose the name of action. Soft you now,
The fair Ophelia. Nymph, in thy orisons
90   Be all my sins remembered.

OPHELIA: Good my lord,
How does your honour for this many a day?

HAMLET: I humbly thank you, well, well, well.

OPHELIA: My lord, I have remembrances of yours
That I have longèd long to re-deliver.
95   I pray you, now receive them.

HAMLET: No, not I!
I never gave you aught.

OPHELIA: My honoured lord, you know right well you did,
And with them words of so sweet breath composed
As made the things more rich. Their perfume lost,
100   Take these again; for to the noble mind
Rich gifts wax poor when givers prove unkind.
There, my lord.

HAMLET: Ha, ha! Are you honest?

OPHELIA: My lord?

105   **HAMLET:** Are you fair?

OPHELIA: What means your lordship?

HAMLET: That if you be honest and fair, your honesty should admit
no discourse to your beauty.

109 *commerce:* dealings
112 *bawd:* brothel-keeper
117 *inoculate our old stock:* be transplanted into our nature
       but we shall relish of it: that we shall be pleased with it
119 *nunnery:* cloister, home for nuns
120 *indifferent honest:* moderately virtuous
123 *beck:* command
126 *arrant knaves:* villainous rascals
133 *dowry:* wedding gift
134 *calumny:* slander, gossip
       if thou wilt needs marry: if you insist on getting married
138 *restore:* bring back to health
139 *paintings:* make-up
141 *jig:* dance
       amble: walk with an exaggerated movement
       lisp: speak in an affected manner
142 *make ... ignorance:* use innocence as an excuse for wilful behaviour

OPHELIA: Could beauty, my lord, have better commerce than with
110   honesty?
HAMLET: Ay, truly, for the power of beauty will sooner transform
       honesty from what it is to a bawd, than the force of honesty can
       translate beauty into his likeness. This was sometime a paradox,
       but now the time gives it proof. I did love you once.
115   **OPHELIA:** Indeed, my lord, you made me believe so.
HAMLET: You should not have believed me, for virtue cannot so
       inoculate our old stock but we shall relish of it. I loved you not.
OPHELIA: I was the more deceived.
HAMLET: Get thee to a nunnery! Why wouldst thou be a breeder of
120   sinners? I am myself indifferent honest, but yet I could accuse
       me of such things, that it were better my mother had not borne
       me. I am very proud, revengeful, ambitious, with more offences
       at my beck than I have thoughts to put them in, imagination
       to give them shape, or time to act them in. What should such
125   fellows as I do crawling between earth and heaven? We are
       arrant knaves all, believe none of us. Go thy ways to a nunnery.
       Where's your father?
OPHELIA: At home, my lord.
HAMLET: Let the doors be shut upon him, that he may play the
130   fool nowhere but in's own house. Farewell.
OPHELIA: O, help him, you sweet heavens!
HAMLET: If thou dost marry, I'll give thee this plague for thy
       dowry: be thou as chaste as ice, as pure as snow, thou shalt not
       escape calumny. Get thee to a nunnery. Go, farewell. Or if thou
135   wilt needs marry, marry a fool, for wise men know well enough
       what monsters you make of them. To a nunnery, go, and quickly
       too. Farewell.
OPHELIA: O heavenly powers, restore him!
HAMLET: I have heard of your paintings too, well enough. God
140   hath given you one face, and you make yourselves another. You
       jig, you amble, and you lisp, you nickname God's creatures and
       make your wantonness your ignorance. Go to, I'll no more on't,
       it hath made me mad. I say, we will have no more marriages.

146 *o'erthrown:* ruined, destroyed
148 *expectancy and rose:* hope and symbol of youth and beauty
149 *glass of fashion:* mirror
mould of form: model
150 *th' observed of all observers:* the one most honoured and respected
151 *deject and wretched:* miserable and devastated
152 *music vows:* melodious promises
153 *sovereign reason:* supreme intellect
155 *blown:* in full bloom
156 *blasted with ecstasy:* destroyed by madness
woe is me: exclamation of grief
158 *affections:* feelings
161 *sits on brood:* sits like a bird on eggs
162 *the hatch and the disclose:* the result
166 *neglected tribute:* payment not yet made
167 *haply:* perhaps
168 *variable objects:* different places of interest
expel: drive out; banish
169 *something-settled:* somewhat fixed
170–171 *brains ... himself:* strange thoughts he is keeping secret make him act unlike himself

Those that are married already – all but one – shall live, the rest
145 shall keep as they are. To a nunnery, go.

Exit.

OPHELIA: O, what a noble mind is here o'erthrown!
   The courtier's, scholar's, soldier's, eye, tongue, sword,
   Th' expectancy and rose of the fair state,
   The glass of fashion and the mould of form,
150 Th' observed of all observers, quite, quite down,
   And I, of ladies most deject and wretched,
   That sucked the honey of his music vows,
   Now see that noble and most sovereign reason,
   Like sweet bells jangled, out of tune and harsh;
155 That unmatched form and feature of blown youth
   Blasted with ecstasy. O, woe is me
   T' have seen what I have seen, see what I see!

Enter KING *and* POLONIUS.

CLAUDIUS: Love? His affections do not that way tend;
   Nor what he spake, though it lacked form a little,
160 Was not like madness. There's something in his soul
   O'er which his melancholy sits on brood,
   And I do doubt the hatch and the disclose
   Will be some danger; which for to prevent,
   I have in quick determination
165 Thus set it down: he shall with speed to England
   For the demand of our neglected tribute.
   Haply the seas, and countries different,
   With variable objects, shall expel
   This something-settled matter in his heart,
170 Whereon his brains still beating puts him thus
   From fashion of himself. What think you on't?

173 *commencement:* beginning
174 *sprung:* originated from
179 *round:* strict
180–181 *placed … conference:* stand in earshot
181 *if she find him not:* if she does not discover his secrets
182 *confine him:* keep him in a closed space

POLONIUS: It shall do well. But yet do I believe
The origin and commencement of his grief
Sprung from neglected love. How now, Ophelia?
175 You need not tell us what Lord Hamlet said.
We heard it all. My lord, do as you please;
But if you hold it fit, after the play,
Let his queen mother all alone entreat him
To show his grief. Let her be round with him,
180 And I'll be placed, so please you, in the ear
Of all their conference. If she find him not,
To England send him; or confine him where
Your wisdom best shall think.
CLAUDIUS: It shall be so.
Madness in great ones must not unwatchèd go.

Exeunt.

Summary:

Hamlet gives notes to the travelling players on how to avoid overacting and asks Horatio to observe Claudius's reaction to the play closely in order to get conclusive evidence for the king's guilt. After the court has entered, Hamlet refuses his mother's request to sit by her and prefers Ophelia's company, whom he harasses with obscene puns. Before the actual play begins, a short mime illustrates its plot with a queen assuring her royal husband of everlasting love before he is poisoned by a murderer who wins the queen's love shortly afterwards. When the actors reach the moment of the poisoning in the full play's spoken version, which re-enacts King Hamlet's murder, Claudius rushes from the room, thus ending the performance. Both Hamlet and Horatio find the ghost's words confirmed and the king guilty. Rosencrantz and Guildenstern inform Hamlet that Gertrude wants to see him in her private room at once and probe him further about his state of mind, which angers Hamlet, who then accuses them of being dishonest with him. Polonius arrives to repeat the queen's order and Hamlet agrees to see her. He is in a bloodthirsty mood and reminds himself not to hurt his mother, as he had promised the ghost.

Annotations:

2 *trippingly:* lightly
   mouth it: declaim it; speak it in an exaggerated manner
3 *as lief:* rather
4 *saw the air:* gesticulate too much (saw = *Säge*)
6 *acquire and beget:* develop, achieve
8 *robustious:* bombastic, loud-mouthed
   periwig-pated (adj): with a wig on his head
9 *groundlings:* poor spectators in the Elizabethan theatre standing in front of the stage (cf. "Shakespeare's Theatre", p. 301)
10 *are capable of:* can understand
   dumb-shows: mimed scenes without dialogue
11–12 *Termagant, Herod:* noisy, raging characters in medieval Mystery Plays
12 *out-Herods Herod:* speaks even more loudly and angrily than Herod
13 *warrant:* will do so; assure
14 *discretion:* judgement
17 *from the purpose of:* far from the intended aim
19–21 *show ... pressure:* i.e. reflect everything truthfully and without distortion
21–22 *come tardy off:* imperfectly done
22–23 *the judicious:* the intelligent ones
23 *censure of the which:* whose judgement
23–24 *allowance:* acceptance, admission
26 *profanely:* in a vulgar way
27 *gait:* manner of walking
28 *strutted:* walked affectedly

Scene II

Elsinore. Hall in the castle.

Enter HAMLET *and three of the* PLAYERS.

HAMLET: Speak the speech, I pray you, as I pronounced it to you,
trippingly on the tongue, but if you mouth it, as many of our
players do, I had as lief the town-crier spoke my lines. Nor do
not saw the air too much with your hand, thus, but use all
5   gently; for in the very torrent, tempest, and, as I may say, whirl-
wind of your passion, you must acquire and beget a temperance
that may give it smoothness. O, it offends me to the soul to hear
a robustious periwig-pated fellow tear a passion to tatters, to
very rags, to split the ears of the groundlings, who for the most
10   part are capable of nothing but inexplicable dumb-shows and
noise. I would have such a fellow whipped for o'erdoing Termagant – it out-Herods Herod. Pray you avoid it.
FIRST PLAYER: I warrant your honour.
HAMLET: Be not too tame neither, but let your own discretion be
15   your tutor. Suit the action to the word, the word to the action,
with this special observance, that you o'erstep not the modesty
of nature. For anything so o'erdone is from the purpose of
playing, whose end both at the first and now, was and is, to
hold as 'twere the mirror up to nature; to show virtue her own
20   feature, scorn her own image, and the very age and body of the
time his form and pressure. Now this overdone, or come tardy
off, though it makes the unskilful laugh, cannot but make the
judicious grieve; the censure of the which one must in your
allowance o'erweigh a whole theatre of others. O, there be
25   players that I have seen play, and heard others praise, and that
highly, not to speak it profanely, that, neither having th' accent
of Christians, nor the gait of Christian, pagan, nor man, have
so strutted and bellowed that I have thought some of nature's

29   *journeymen:* unskilled workmen
30   *abominably:* terribly; unnaturally
31   *reformed:* improved
       indifferently: quite well
35   *some quantity:* a number, some
36   *barren:* dull, apathetic
41   *presently:* very soon
48   *as e'er … coped withal:* as I have ever met

30 journeymen had made men, and not made them well, they
imitated humanity so abominably.

FIRST PLAYER: I hope we have reformed that indifferently with us,
sir.

HAMLET: O, reform it altogether. And let those that play your
clowns speak no more than is set down for them, for there be
35 of them that will themselves laugh, to set on some quantity of
barren spectators to laugh too, though in the meantime some
necessary question of the play be then to be considered. That's
villainous and shows a most pitiful ambition in the fool that
uses it. Go make you ready.

Exeunt PLAYERS.

Enter POLONIUS, ROSENCRANTZ *and* GUILDENSTERN.

40 How now, my lord? Will the king hear this piece of work?
POLONIUS: And the queen too, and that presently.
HAMLET: Bid the players make haste.

Exit POLONIUS.

Will you two help to hasten them?
ROSENCRANTZ: ⎫
                 ⎬ We will, my lord.
GUILDENSTERN: ⎭

Exeunt ROSENCRANTZ *and* GUILDENSTERN.

45 **HAMLET:** What, ho, Horatio!

Enter HORATIO.

HORATIO: Here, sweet lord, at your service.
HAMLET: Horatio, thou art e'en as just a man
As e'er my conversation coped withal.

50 *advancement:* advantage
51 *revenue:* income
53 *candied tongue:* flattering speech
    lick absurd pomp: flatter people in high positions
54 *crook ... knees:* bend your knees
55 *thrift:* profit, reward
    fawning: flattery
57 *distinguish her election:* find a choice
58 *sh'ath sealed thee:* she has chosen you
59 *in suffering ... nothing:* suffering without complaint
60 *buffets:* blows
61 *ta'en:* taken
62 *blood:* passion
    commeddled: mixed together
64 *sound what stop:* play what melody
66 *core:* centre
67 *something too much of this:* I talk too much
71 *prithee:* beg you, ask you
    afoot: in progress
72 *very comment:* absolute concentration
73 *occulted:* hidden
74 *unkennel:* make known
75 *damnèd:* devilish
76 *foul:* black, disorderly
77 *Vulcan's stithy:* the ancient god of fire's workshop
    heedful note: careful attention
78 *rivet:* cling closely
79 *after:* afterwards
80 *censure of his scheming:* judgement of his behaviour

HORATIO: O, my dear lord!

HAMLET: Nay, do not think I flatter;

50 For what advancement may I hope from thee,
That no revenue hast but thy good spirits
To feed and clothe thee? Why should the poor be flattered?
No, let the candied tongue lick absurd pomp,
And crook the pregnant hinges of the knee

55 Where thrift may follow fawning. Dost thou hear?
Since my dear soul was mistress of her choice
And could of men distinguish her election
Sh'ath sealed thee for herself. For thou hast been
As one in suffering all that suffers nothing,

60 A man that Fortune's buffets and rewards
Hast ta'en with equal thanks. And blest are those
Whose blood and judgement are so well commeddled
That they are not a pipe for Fortune's finger
To sound what stop she please. Give me that man

65 That is not passion's slave, and I will wear him
In my heart's core, ay, in my heart of heart,
As I do thee. Something too much of this.
There is a play tonight before the king:
One scene of it comes near the circumstance

70 Which I have told thee of my father's death.
I prithee, when thou seest that act afoot,
Even with the very comment of thy soul
Observe my uncle. If his occulted guilt
Do not itself unkennel in one speech,

75 It is a damnèd ghost that we have seen,
And my imaginations are as foul
As Vulcan's stithy. Give him heedful note,
For I mine eyes will rivet to his face,
And after we will both our judgements join

80 In censure of his seeming.

81 *steals aught:* hides anything
82 *'scape detecting:* is not found out
   I will pay the theft: I shall be responsible
83 *idle:* seem unoccupied
85 *fares:* 1. does; 2. eats
86 *i' faith:* indeed
   of the chameleon's dish: i.e. air (chameleons were thought to feed on air)
87 *promise-crammed:* full of promise
   capons: castrated male chickens made fat for meals
88 *I have nothing with:* I cannot make sense of
92 *accounted:* thought of as, considered
94 *Capitol:* seat of government in Rome where Julius Caesar was assassinated
95 *Brutus:* Roman senator who conspired against Caesar and took part in his
   murder

Note, ll. 94–96: Hamlet mocks Polonius with wordplay (*brute – Brutus*, *capital –*
   Capitol and *calf* = fool).

 98 *stay upon your patience:* wait for your permission
100 *attractive:* with magnetic powers
102 *shall I lie in your lap:* recline upon you, have sex with you
106 *country matters:* sexual intercourse

HORATIO: Well, my lord.
　　If he steals aught the whilst this play is playing,
　　And 'scape detecting, I will pay the theft.

*Sound a flourish. Enter trumpets and kettledrums. Danish march.
Enter* KING, QUEEN, POLONIUS, OPHELIA, ROSENCRANTZ, GUIL-
DENSTERN *and other* LORDS *attendant, with the* GUARD *carrying
torches.*

HAMLET: They are coming to the play. I must be idle.
　　Get you a place.
85　**CLAUDIUS:** How fares our cousin Hamlet?
　　HAMLET: Excellent, i' faith, of the chameleon's dish: I eat the air,
　　　promise-crammed. You cannot feed capons so.
　　CLAUDIUS: I have nothing with this answer, Hamlet, these words
　　　are not mine.
90　**HAMLET:** No, nor mine now. *[To* POLONIUS*]* My lord, you played
　　　once i' th' university, you say?
　　POLONIUS: That did I, my lord, and was accounted a good actor.
　　HAMLET: What did you enact?
　　POLONIUS: I did enact Julius Caesar. I was killed i' th' Capitol.
95　　Brutus killed me.
　　HAMLET: It was a brute part of him to kill so capital a calf there. –
　　　Be the players ready?
　　ROSENCRANTZ: Ay, my lord. They stay upon your patience.
　　GERTRUDE: Come hither, my dear Hamlet, sit by me.
100　**HAMLET:** No, good mother. Here's metal more attractive.
　　POLONIUS: *[To the* KING*]* O, ho! Do you mark that?
　　HAMLET: Lady, shall I lie in your lap?
　　OPHELIA: No, my lord.
　　HAMLET: I mean, my head upon your lap?
105　**OPHELIA:** Ay, my lord.
　　HAMLET: Do you think I meant country matters?
　　OPHELIA: I think nothing, my lord.
　　HAMLET: That's a fair thought to lie between maids' legs.

114 *jig-maker:* comedian
119 *sables:* dark fur (*Pelz*) worn at funerals
121 *by'r Lady:* by Our Lady, i.e. the Virgin Mary
122 *shall he suffer not thinking on:* will he have to accept that he will be forgotten
hobby-horse: feature in a popular dance and in a song, from which Hamlet
proceeds to quote (*Steckenpferd*)
123 *epitaph:* inscription on a gravestone
- *dumb-show:* mime
makes show of protestations unto him: solemnly declares her love to him
declines: leans
anon: soon afterwards
makes passionate action: makes gestures of extreme grief
mutes: other silent players
condole: express sorrow
woos: persuades her to love him
125 *miching mallecho: heimlicher Unfug*
126 *belike:* it seems
imports the argument: sums up the plot
prologue: actor introducing the play

OPHELIA: What is, my lord?

110 **HAMLET:** Nothing.

OPHELIA: You are merry, my lord.

HAMLET: Who, I?

OPHELIA: Ay, my lord.

HAMLET: O God, your only jig-maker. What should a man do but
115   be merry? For look you how cheerfully my mother looks, and
         my father died within 's two hours.

OPHELIA: Nay, 'tis twice two months, my lord.

HAMLET: So long? Nay then, let the devil wear black, for I'll have a
         suit of sables. O heavens! Die two months ago, and not forgot-
120   ten yet? Then there's hope a great man's memory may outlive
         his life half a year. But, by'r Lady, he must build churches then,
         or else shall he suffer not thinking on, with the hobby-horse,
         whose epitaph is 'For O, for O, the hobby-horse is forgot!'

Trumpets sound. The dumb-show enters.
Enter a king and a queen very lovingly, the queen embracing him and
he her. She kneels and makes show of protestation unto him. He takes
her up, and declines his head upon her neck. He lays him down upon
a bank of flowers. She, seeing him asleep, leaves him. Anon comes in a
fellow, takes off his crown, kisses it, pours poison in the sleeper's ears,
and leaves him. The queen returns, finds the king dead, and makes
passionate action. The poisoner with some three or four mutes, comes
in again, seeming to condole with her. The dead body is carried away.
The poisoner woos the queen with gifts. She seems harsh and unwill-
ing awhile, but in the end accepts his love.

Exeunt.

OPHELIA: What means this, my lord?

125 **HAMLET:** Marry, this is miching mallecho; it means mischief.

OPHELIA: Belike this show imports the argument of the play?

Enter Prologue.

127–128 *keep counsel:* keep a secret

132 *naught:* rude, indecent
mark: pay attention to

Note, ll. 129–132: Hamlet keeps giving the word 'show' a sexual meaning, which Ophelia refuses to acknowledge.

134 *stooping to your clemency:* submitting to your kindness

136 *posy of a ring:* short motto engraved inside a ring

139 *Phoebus' cart:* i.e. the sun; the sun god Phoebus was thought to drive a carriage with fiery horses

140 *Neptune's salt wash:* i.e. the sea, of which Neptune is the god
Tellus' orbèd ground: i.e. the earth, of which Tellus is the goddess

141 *borrowed sheen:* brightness reflected from the sun

142 *times twelve thirties:* 30 years

143 *Hymen:* god of marriage

144 *unite ... bands:* joined (our hands) in marriage

146 *ere:* before

149 *distrust:* worry about

150 *discomfort ... must:* do not let this upset you

151 *holds quantity:* are equal in relation to each other

152 *in neither ... extremity:* either too much or too little

153 *proof:* experience

154 *sized:* beyond limits

HAMLET: We shall know by this fellow. The players cannot keep
counsel, they'll tell all.

OPHELIA: Will he tell us what this show meant?

130 **HAMLET:** Ay, or any show that you'll show him. Be not you
ashamed to show, he'll not shame to tell you what it means.

OPHELIA: You are naught, you are naught. I'll mark the play.

PROLOGUE: *For us, and for our tragedy,*
Here stooping to your clemency,
135 *We beg your hearing patiently.*

Exit.

HAMLET: Is this a prologue, or the posy of a ring?

OPHELIA: 'Tis brief, my lord.

HAMLET: As woman's love.

Enter the PLAYER KING *and* QUEEN.

PLAYER KING: *Full thirty times hath Phoebus' cart gone round*
140 *Neptune's salt wash and Tellus' orbèd ground,*
And thirty dozen moons with borrowed sheen
About the world have times twelve thirties been,
Since love our hearts, and Hymen did our hands,
Unite commutual in most sacred bands.

145 **PLAYER QUEEN:** *So many journeys may the sun and moon*
Make us again count o'er ere love be done.
But woe is me, you are so sick of late,
So far from cheer and from your former state,
That I distrust you. Yet, though I distrust,
150 *Discomfort you, my lord, it nothing must.*
For women's fear and love holds quantity,
In neither aught, or in extremity.
Now what my love is, proof hath made you know;
And as my love is sized, my fear is so.

158 *my ... to do:* my senses (sight, hearing etc.) fail to function
159 *behind:* when I am dead
160 *haply:* fortunately
161 *confound:* stop
162 *needs:* necessarily
163 *accurst:* doomed to misery
164 *none ... first:* if she takes a second husband, she killed the first
165 *wormwood:* bitter
166 *instances:* motives
      move: bring about
167 *base respects of thrift:* financial reasons
172 *purpose ... memory:* resolutions are worn away by time
173 *of ... validity:* strongly felt at first but not lasting
175 *mellow:* soft with ripeness
176–177 *most necessary ... debt:* we will forget to keep our promises to ourselves
178–179 *the passion ... lose:* once our emotion ends, we forget our promises
181 *enactures:* actions
183 *grief ... accident:* one extreme feeling will turn into its opposite at the slightest event
184 *is not for aye:* does not last forever
187 *lead:* controls
188 *his favourite flies:* the person favoured by him deserts him

155 *Where love is great, the littlest doubts are fear;*
  Where little fears grow great, great love grows there.
  PLAYER KING: *Faith, I must leave thee, love, and shortly too;*
    My operant powers their functions leave to do.
    And thou shalt live in this fair world behind,
160 *Honoured, beloved, and haply one as kind*
    For husband shalt thou –
  PLAYER QUEEN: *O, confound the rest!*
    Such love must needs be treason in my breast.
    When second husband let me be accurst!
    None wed the second but who killed the first.
165 **HAMLET:** *[Aside]* Wormwood, wormwood!
  PLAYER QUEEN: *The instances that second marriage move*
    Are base respects of thrift, but none of love.
    A second time I kill my husband dead
    When second husband kisses me in bed.
170 **PLAYER KING:** *I do believe you think what now you speak,*
    But what we do determine oft we break.
    Purpose is but the slave to memory,
    Of violent birth, but poor validity,
    Which now, like fruit unripe, sticks on the tree,
175 *But fall unshaken when they mellow be.*
    Most necessary 'tis that we forget
    To pay ourselves what to ourselves is debt.
    What to ourselves in passion we propose,
    The passion ending, doth the purpose lose.
180 *The violence of either grief or joy*
    Their own enactures with themselves destroy.
    Where joy most revels, grief doth most lament;
    Grief joys, joy grieves, on slender accident.
    This world is not for aye, nor 'tis not strange
185 *That even our loves should with our fortunes change,*
    For 'tis a question left us yet to prove,
    Whether love lead fortune, or else fortune love.
    The great man down, you mark his favourite flies,

189 *the poor advanced:* the poor man raised to a higher position
190 *hitherto:* up to this point
  tend: serves
191 *not needs:* is rich
192 *in want:* needs help
  hollow: false
  try: ask for help
193 *seasons him:* turns him into
194 *orderly to end where I begun:* to come back to my original point
195 *contrary* [kən'treəri]: behaving badly, doing the opposite of what is to be expected
196 *devices:* plans
  still: always
197 *ends:* outcomes
199 *die thy thoughts:* your opinion will change
200 *nor:* let neither
201 *sport and repose:* entertainment and sleep
  lock: take away
203 *anchor's cheer:* food/condition of a hermit (*Einsiedler*)
  scope: future
204 *blanks the face of joy:* turns a happy face into a sad one
205 *meet ... destroy:* may it destroy everything dear to me
206 *here and hence:* in this world and the next
  pursue me lasting strife: may I never have peace
210–211 *fain ... sleep:* I would gladly escape this long day and sleep
211 *sleep rock thy brain:* sleep tight
212 *mischance:* bad luck
  us twain: the two of us
214 *doth protest too much:* exaggerates, is over the top
  methinks: it seems to me
216 *argument:* what the play deals with
  offence: harm

The poor advanced makes friends of enemies,
190 And hitherto doth love on fortune tend;
For who not needs shall never lack a friend,
And who in want a hollow friend doth try
Directly seasons him his enemy.
But, orderly to end where I begun,
195 Our wills and fates do so contrary run
That our devices still are overthrown;
Our thoughts are ours, their ends none of our own.
So think thou wilt no second husband wed;
But die thy thoughts when thy first lord is dead.
200 **PLAYER QUEEN:** *Nor earth to me give food, nor heaven light,*
Sport and repose lock from me day and night,
To desperation turn my trust and hope,
An anchor's cheer in prison be my scope,
Each opposite that blanks the face of joy
205 Meet what I would have well, and it destroy,
Both here and hence pursue me lasting strife,
If, once a widow, ever I be wife.
HAMLET: If she should break it now!
PLAYER KING: *'Tis deeply sworn. Sweet, leave me here awhile.*
210 My spirits grow dull, and fain I would beguile
The tedious day with sleep.
PLAYER QUEEN: Sleep rock thy brain,

He sleeps.

PLAYER QUEEN: *And never come mischance between us twain.*

Exit.

HAMLET: Madam, how like you this play?
GERTRUDE: The lady doth protest too much, methinks.
215 **HAMLET:** O, but she'll keep her word.
CLAUDIUS: Have you heard the argument? Is there no offence in't?

217 *jest:* pretend
220 *tropically:* figuratively
222 *knavish:* pleasant and funny but looking as if something be might be wrong
223–224 *free souls:* a clear conscience
224 *galled jade:* horse that has a sore (from an ill-fitting saddle)
    wince: kick out from pain
    withers: shoulders
225 *unwrung:* unhurt
227 *chorus:* actor who interpreted part of the play
229 *puppets:* 1. figures in a puppet show; 2. (figurative) male sexual organs
    dallying: making love
230 *keen:* intellectually sharp
231 *cost you a groaning:* make you cry
    edge: strong sexual desire
232 *better and worse:* wittier, but objectionable
233 *so:* in such a way
    mistake: betray; fool with false promises
    pox: (slight curse) plague
234 *damnable faces:* excessive facial expressions
234–235 *croaking ... revenge:* Hamlet quotes from an old play
236 *apt:* fit and ready
    drugs fit: poisons ready
237 *confederate season:* perfect time
238 *rank:* foul, stinking
    midnight weeds: toxic herbs collected at midnight
239 *Hecate's ban:* queen of the witches' curse
    thrice blasted: bewitched three times
240 *dire property:* dreadful nature
241 *wholesome:* healthy
    usurp: destroy
242 *for his estate:* for his land and title
243 *is extant:* still exists
    choice: fine
244 *anon:* very soon

HAMLET: No, no, they do but jest, poison in jest, no offence i' th'
world.

CLAUDIUS: What do you call the play?

220 **HAMLET:** 'The Mousetrap'. Marry, how? Tropically. This play is
the image of a murder done in Vienna. Gonzago is the duke's
name, his wife, Baptista. You shall see anon. 'Tis a knavish piece
of work, but what o' that? Your Majesty, and we that have free
souls, it touches us not. Let the galled jade wince; our withers
225 are unwrung.

Enter LUCIANUS.

This is one Lucianus, nephew to the king.

OPHELIA: You are as good as a chorus, my lord.

HAMLET: I could interpret between you and your love, if I could
see the puppets dallying.

230 **OPHELIA:** You are keen, my lord, you are keen.

HAMLET: It would cost you a groaning to take off mine edge.

OPHELIA: Still better, and worse.

HAMLET: So you mis-take your husbands. Begin, murderer. Pox,
leave thy damnable faces, and begin! Come, the croaking raven
235 doth bellow for revenge.

LUCIANUS: *Thoughts black, hands apt, drugs fit, and time agreeing,*
Confederate season, else no creature seeing.
Thou mixture rank, of midnight weeds collected,
With Hecate's ban thrice blasted, thrice infected,
240 *Thy natural magic and dire property*
On wholesome life usurp immediately.

Pours the poison in the PLAYERS KING's *ears.*

HAMLET: He poisons him i' th' garden for his estate. His name's
Gonzago. The story is extant, and written in very choice Italian.
You shall see anon how the murderer gets the love of Gonzago's
245 wife.

247 *frighted with false fire:* scared by blank ammunition
249 *give o'er:* stop
252 *strucken:* wounded
  deer: Rotwild
248 *hart: Hirsch*
  ungallèd: uninjured
255 *thus runs the world away:* that is how the world goes
256 *forest of feathers:* exotic dress with feathers worn by actors
257 *turn Turk:* change for the worse
  provincial roses: rosettes on shoes hiding shoelaces
258 *razed shoes:* shoes with ornamental cuts
  fellowship: membership; percentage of the entrance fee
  cry: company
261 *Damon:* allusion to the Greek tale of Damon's and Pythias's legendary
  friendship
262 *realm* [relm]: kingdom
  dismantled: destroyed, ruined
263 *Jove:* Jupiter/Zeus, king of the gods, i.e. Claudius
264 *pajock:* peacock (*Pfau*)

Note, l. 264: The missing rhyme for 'was' that Horatio mentions might be 'ass'
  (*Esel*).

267 *didst perceive:* did you notice
271 *recorders:* flutes
273 *belike:* it seems
  perdy: by God (from French par dieu)

OPHELIA: The king rises.

HAMLET: What, frighted with false fire?

GERTRUDE: How fares my lord?

POLONIUS: Give o'er the play.

250 **CLAUDIUS:** Give me some light! Away!

LORDS: Lights, lights, lights!

Exeunt all but HAMLET *and* HORATIO.

HAMLET: Why, let the strucken deer go weep,
          The hart ungallèd play;
       For some must watch, while some must sleep,
255   Thus runs the world away.
    Would not this, sir, and a forest of feathers, if the rest of my
    fortunes turn Turk with me, with two provincial roses on my
    razed shoes, get me a fellowship in a cry of players, sir?

HORATIO: Half a share.

260 **HAMLET:** A whole one I!
          For thou dost know, O Damon dear,
            This realm dismantled was
          Of Jove himself; and now reigns here
             A very, very – pajock.

265 **HORATIO:** You might have rhymed.

HAMLET: O good Horatio, I'll take the ghost's word for a thousand
    pound. Didst perceive?

HORATIO: Very well, my lord.

HAMLET: Upon the talk of the poisoning?

270 **HORATIO:** I did very well note him.

HAMLET: Aha! Come, some music! Come, the recorders!
    For if the king like not the comedy,
    Why then, belike he likes it not, perdy.
    Come, some music!

Enter ROSENCRANTZ *and* GUILDENSTERN.

275 *vouchsafe:* grant, allow
279 *retirement:* withdrawal to his private room
    marvellous distempered: greatly disturbed, out of humour
281 *choler:* anger, one of the 'four humours' thought to be ruling one's
    temperament
282 *signify:* communicate
283 *purgation:* cure, cleansing by bloodletting
284 *plunge ... choler:* make him even angrier
285 *discourse:* talk
286 *frame:* order
    start not so wildly: be not so hasty
    my affair: my business; what I have to tell you
287 *I am tame, sir, pronounce:* I will listen patiently, sir, speak
288 *affliction:* severe suffering
292 *breed:* kind, manner
    wholesome: suitable
294 *pardon:* permission
302 *amazement:* alarm
    admiration: great surprise
303 *stonish:* astonish
304 *sequel at the heels:* consequence
305 *impart:* tell
306 *closet* ['klɒzɪt]: bedroom, private room
309 *trade:* dealings, business

275 **GUILDENSTERN:** Good my lord, vouchsafe me a word with you.

HAMLET: Sir, a whole history.

GUILDENSTERN: The king, sir –

HAMLET: Ay, sir, what of him?

GUILDENSTERN: Is in his retirement marvellous distempered.

280 **HAMLET:** With drink, sir?

GUILDENSTERN: No, my lord; rather with choler.

HAMLET: Your wisdom should show itself more richer to signify
this to the doctor; for, for me to put him to his purgation would
perhaps plunge him into far more choler.

285 **GUILDENSTERN:** Good my lord, put your discourse into some
frame, and start not so wildly from my affair.

HAMLET: I am tame, sir; pronounce.

GUILDENSTERN: The queen your mother, in most great affliction
of spirit, hath sent me to you.

290 **HAMLET:** You are welcome.

GUILDENSTERN: Nay, good my lord, this courtesy is not of the
right breed. If it shall please you to make me a wholesome
answer, I will do your mother's commandment; if not, your
pardon and my return shall be the end of my business.

295 **HAMLET:** Sir, I cannot.

GUILDENSTERN: What, my lord?

HAMLET: Make you a wholesome answer; my wit's diseased. But,
sir, such answer as I can make, you shall command, or rather, as
you say, my mother. Therefore no more, but to the matter. My
300 mother, you say.

ROSENCRANTZ: Then thus she says: your behaviour hath struck
her into amazement and admiration.

HAMLET: O wonderful son that can so stonish a mother! But
is there no sequel at the heels of this mother's admiration?
305 Impart.

ROSENCRANTZ: She desires to speak with you in her closet ere you
go to bed.

HAMLET: We shall obey, were she ten times our mother. Have you
any further trade with us?

311 *pickers and stealers:* hands (i.e. 'I still do')
312 *distemper:* angry mood; mental derangement
313 *bar:* shut with a bolt
         deny: refuse to tell
315 *advancement:* ambition to rule Denmark
317 *succession:* becoming the next king
318 *proverb:* common saying
319 *musty:* stale, tasteless (the full proverb says 'While the grass grows, the horse starves')
320 *withdraw:* speak privately
321 *recover the wind of me:* find out my innermost secrets
322 *toil:* net

Note, ll. 321–322: Hamlet's imagery is taken from hunting, where hunters avoid being smelled by their prey.

323–324 *if my duty … unmannerly:* if my behaviour is too rude, it is my love for you that is to blame
330 *beseech:* beg
332 *govern these ventages:* cover these holes
334 *discourse:* play
         eloquent: melodious
         stops: holes
335 *utterance:* sound
339 *mystery:* innermost thoughts
340 *sound:* question; produce music
         compass: range

310 **ROSENCRANTZ:** My lord, you once did love me.

HAMLET: And do still, by these pickers and stealers.

ROSENCRANTZ: Good my lord, what is your cause of distemper?
You do surely bar the door upon your own liberty, if you deny
your griefs to your friend.

315 **HAMLET:** Sir, I lack advancement.

ROSENCRANTZ: How can that be, when you have the voice of the
king himself for your succession in Denmark?

HAMLET: Ay, sir, but 'while the grass grows' – the proverb is something musty.

Enter the PLAYERS *with recorders.*

320 O, the recorders! Let me see one. To withdraw with you – why
do you go about to recover the wind of me, as if you would drive
me into a toil?

GUILDENSTERN: O my lord, if my duty be too bold, my love is too
unmannerly.

325 **HAMLET:** I do not well understand that. Will you play upon this
pipe?

GUILDENSTERN: My lord, I cannot.

HAMLET: I pray you.

GUILDENSTERN: Believe me, I cannot.

330 **HAMLET:** I do beseech you.

GUILDENSTERN: I know no touch of it, my lord.

HAMLET: It is as easy as lying. Govern these ventages with your
fingers and thumbs, give it breath with your mouth, and it will
discourse most eloquent music. Look you, these are the stops.

335 **GUILDENSTERN:** But these cannot I command to any utterance of
harmony. I have not the skill.

HAMLET: Why, look you now, how unworthy a thing you make
of me. You would play upon me, you would seem to know my
stops, you would pluck out the heart of my mystery, you would

340 sound me from my lowest note to the top of my compass – and
there is much music, excellent voice, in this little organ, yet

342 *'sblood:* exclamation: by God's *blood*
344 *fret:* irritate
346–347 *presently:* straight away
348 *yonder:* over there
350 *by th' mass:* (exclamation) by the Roman Catholic Mass
351 *weasel: Wiesel*
355 *by and by:* soon
356 *to the top of my bent:* to the utmost limit
359 *witching time:* time when witches, ghosts and wizards rule
361 *contagion:* evil; pestilential matter
363 *quake:* tremble with fear
        soft: careful
364 *nature:* natural feelings
365 *Nero:* Roman emperor who had his own mother killed
        firm bosom: strong chest

cannot you make it speak. 'Sblood, do you think I am easier to
be played on than a pipe? Call me what instrument you will,
though you can fret me, you cannot play upon me.

Enter POLONIUS.

345 God bless you, sir!
POLONIUS: My lord, the queen would speak with you, and pres-
ently.
HAMLET: Do you see yonder cloud that's almost in shape of a
camel?
350 **POLONIUS:** By th' mass, and 'tis like a camel indeed.
HAMLET: Methinks it is like a weasel.
POLONIUS: It is backed like a weasel.
HAMLET: Or like a whale.
POLONIUS: Very like a whale.
355 **HAMLET:** Then will I come to my mother by and by. – They fool me
to the top of my bent. – I will come by and by.
POLONIUS: I will say so.

Exit.

HAMLET: By and by is easily said. – Leave me, friends.

Exeunt all but HAMLET.

'Tis now the very witching time of night,
360 When churchyards yawn, and hell itself breathes out
Contagion to this world. Now could I drink hot blood,
And do such bitter business as the day
Would quake to look on. Soft! Now to my mother!
O heart, lose not thy nature; let not ever
365 The soul of Nero enter this firm bosom.
Let me be cruel, not unnatural:
I will speak daggers to her, but use none.

368 *be hypocrites:* are different from each other
369 *how ... shent:* however much I criticize and shame her verbally
370 *give them seals:* act upon them
　　consent: agree to

My tongue and soul in this be hypocrites,
How in my words somever she be shent,
370 To give them seals never my soul consent.

Exit.

Summary:

Claudius instructs Rosencrantz and Guildenstern to depart to England with Hamlet and to watch him during their journey. Polonius informs the king that he will hide in Gertrude's room to spy on her conversation with Hamlet. Alone, Claudius feels remorse for murdering his brother and tries to pray, but admits to himself that he cannot expect forgiveness for his crime when he is not ready to give up what he gained by his deed, namely the crown and his wife. Hamlet is now ready to kill Claudius with his sword but delays it because his uncle will go to heaven if killed while praying. Thus, Hamlet decides to do it when Claudius's actions are likely to send him to hell. Ironically, Hamlet has missed a fitting moment because his uncle stopped his prayers since they were not heartfelt.

Annotations:

1   *him:* i.e. his behaviour
stands: is
2   *range:* run wild
3   *commission:* letter of instruction
forthwith dispatch: deal with promptly
5   *terms of our estate:* responsibilities of my position as king
5–6   *endure hazard:* risk danger
6–7   *doth … brows:* as he grows crazier by the hour
7   *provide:* prepare
8   *fear:* concern
11   *single and peculiar:* individual and private
13   *noyance:* harm
14   *spirit:* monarch
weal: welfare, health
15   *cess:* death
16   *gulf:* whirlpool
17   *massy:* massive, huge (cf. Note II, ii, 453]
18   *mount:* mountain
19   *spokes:* bars of a wheel (*Speichen*)
20   *mortised and adjoined:* securely attached
21   *annexment:* appendage, hanger-on
petty consequence: unimportant attachment
22   *attends:* accompanies
boisterous: turbulent
23   *a general groan:* everyone's sorrow
24   *arm you:* make preparations
25   *fetters:* chains

Scene III

A room in the castle.

Enter KING, ROSENCRANTZ, *and* GUILDENSTERN.

CLAUDIUS: I like him not, nor stands it safe with us
    To let his madness range. Therefore prepare you:
    I your commission will forthwith dispatch,
    And he to England shall along with you.
5   The terms of our estate may not endure
    Hazard so near us as doth hourly grow
    Out of his brows.
GUILDENSTERN: We will ourselves provide.
    Most holy and religious fear it is
    To keep those many many bodies safe
10   That live and feed upon your Majesty.
ROSENCRANTZ: The single and peculiar life is bound
    With all the strength and armour of the mind
    To keep itself from noyance; but much more
    That spirit upon whose weal depends and rests
15   The lives of many. The cess of majesty
    Dies not alone, but like a gulf doth draw
    What's near it with it. It is a massy wheel,
    Fixed on the summit of the highest mount,
    To whose huge spokes ten thousand lesser things
20   Are mortised and adjoined; which when it falls,
    Each small annexment, petty consequence,
    Attends the boisterous ruin. Never alone
    Did the king sigh, but with a general groan.
CLAUDIUS: Arm you, I pray you, to this speedy voyage,
25   For we will fetters put upon this fear,
    Which now goes too free-footed.
ROSENCRANTZ: We will haste us.

27   *closet* [ˈklɒzɪt]: bedroom, private room
28   *arras* [ˈærəs]: tapestry hanging on the wall
     convey: hide
29   *tax him home:* criticize him thoroughly
31   *meet* (adj): fitting
32   *partial:* tending to show favour
33   *of vantage:* in addition
36   *rank:* foul-smelling, rotten
37   *primal eldest curse:* (in the Bible) God's curse for Cain who killed his brother
     Abel
39   *inclination … will:* desire and determination are equally strong
40   *defeats:* is stronger than
     intent: intention; aim
41   *bound:* sworn
43   *both neglect:* act on neither of them
46   *whereto:* to what end
47   *confront the visage of offence:* stand up to sin face to face
48   *two-fold:* double
49   *forestallèd:* prevented
50   *then I'll look up:* so I will pray
51   *my fault is past:* I have already committed my sin
52   *turn:* need
53   *I am still possessed:* I still own

Exeunt ROSENCRANTZ *and* GUILDENSTERN.

Enter POLONIUS.

POLONIUS: My lord, he's going to his mother's closet.
    Behind the arras I'll convey myself
    To hear the process. I'll warrant she'll tax him home,
30   And, as you said, and wisely was it said,
    'Tis meet that some more audience than a mother,
    Since nature makes them partial, should o'erhear
    The speech, of vantage. Fare you well, my liege.
    I'll call upon you ere you go to bed
35   And tell you what I know.
CLAUDIUS: Thanks, dear my lord.

Exit POLONIUS.

    O, my offence is rank, it smells to heaven;
    It hath the primal eldest curse upon't,
    A brother's murder. Pray can I not,
    Though inclination be as sharp as will.
40   My stronger guilt defeats my strong intent,
    And, like a man to double business bound,
    I stand in pause where I shall first begin,
    And both neglect. What if this cursèd hand
    Were thicker than itself with brother's blood,
45   Is there not rain enough in the sweet heavens
    To wash it white as snow? Whereto serves mercy
    But to confront the visage of offence?
    And what's in prayer but this two-fold force,
    To be forestallèd ere we come to fall,
50   Or pardoned being down? Then I'll look up;
    My fault is past. But, O, what form of prayer
    Can serve my turn? 'Forgive me my foul murder'?
    That cannot be, since I am still possessed

54 *effects:* benefits
56 *retain th'offence:* keep the profits gained
57 *corrupted currents:* wicked practices
58 *gilded:* bearing gold
 shove by: push to one side
59 *wicked prize:* profits gained by criminal means
60 *buys out:* buys off, bribes
60–61 *above; there:* in heaven
61 *shuffling:* deceit, evasion
 the action lies: the sin is laid bare
62 *compelled:* forced
63–64 *even … evidence:* to confess our worst sins
64 *what rests:* what is the alternative
65 *repentance:* showing that one is sorry for what one has done
68 *limèd:* trapped, caught
69 *art more engaged:* is trapped even more securely
 make assay: help me
70 *stubborn:* unwilling
71 *sinews:* bands that join a muscle to the bone (*Sehnen*)
73 *pat:* instantly; easily
 a-praying: in the act of praying
75 *would be scanned:* should be considered with care
77 *sole:* only
79 *hire and salary:* payment
80 *took my father grossly:* killed my father when he was unprepared for heaven
81 *as flush:* full of life
82 *how … heaven:* only God knows how many sins he has committed
83 *circumstance … thought:* case and way of thinking

Of those effects for which I did the murder,
55   My crown, mine own ambition, and my queen.
May one be pardoned and retain th' offence?
In the corrupted currents of this world
Offence's gilded hand may shove by justice,
And oft 'tis seen the wicked prize itself
60   Buys out the law. But 'tis not so above;
There is no shuffling, there the action lies
In his true nature, and we ourselves compelled,
Even to the teeth and forehead of our faults
To give in evidence. What then? What rests?
65   Try what repentance can. What can it not?
Yet what can it when one cannot repent?
O wretched state! O bosom black as death!
O limèd soul, that struggling to be free
Art more engaged! Help, angels! Make assay:
70   Bow, stubborn knees, and heart with strings of steel
Be soft as sinews of the new-born babe.
All may be well.

He kneels.

Enter HAMLET.

HAMLET: Now might I do it pat, now he is a-praying,
And now I'll do't. And so he goes to heaven,
75   And so am I revenged. That would be scanned.
A villain kills my father; and for that,
I, his sole son, do this same villain send
To heaven.
Why, this is hire and salary, not revenge.
80   He took my father grossly, full of bread,
With all his crimes broad blown, as flush as May,
And how his audit stands, who knows save heaven?
But in our circumstance and course of thought

84   *heavy with him:* difficult for him
85   *take:* kill
         purging: cleansing (being forgiven while praying)
86   *fit and seasoned:* ready, prepared
         passage: journey
88   *up:* away
         horrid hent: fearful opportunity
91   *gaming:* gambling
92   *relish:* taste
95   *stays:* is waiting
96   *physic:* medicine; i.e. Claudius's prayer or Hamlet's decision

'Tis heavy with him. And am I then revenged,
85   To take him in the purging of his soul,
When he is fit and seasoned for his passage?
No.
Up, sword, and know thou a more horrid hent.
When he is drunk asleep, or in his rage,
90   Or in th' incestuous pleasure of his bed,
At gaming, swearing, or about some act
That has no relish of salvation in't –
Then trip him that his heels may kick at heaven,
And that his soul may be as damned and black
95   As hell whereto it goes. My mother stays.
This physic but prolongs thy sickly days.

Exit.

CLAUDIUS: *[Rises]* My words fly up, my thoughts remain below.
Words without thoughts never to heaven go.

Exit.

Summary:

In the queen's private room, Polonius advises Gertrude to be strict with Hamlet. He then goes to hide behind a tapestry to eavesdrop. Gertrude intends to berate Hamlet for his behaviour and is astonished when he attacks her for marrying Claudius. Hamlet is so agitated that she cries out in fear for her life, which causes Polonius to reveal his presence by calling for help. Believing it is the king, Hamlet stabs Polonius through the tapestry and remains unmoved when he finds out about his error. Continuing his reproaches, he asks his mother how she could have chosen Claudius, who murdered his brother, after having been married to the excellent king that was his father. Gertrude tries in vain to stop Hamlet's rantings when the ghost appears and reminds him that he should focus on his revenge and not bother his mother. Gertrude, who cannot see the apparition, thinks that her son is stark raving mad and promises to do everything he demands of her, especially not to have sexual relations with Claudius. Finally, Hamlet remembers his trip to England, wishes Gertrude good night and pulls Polonius's body out of the room.

Annotations:

  1 *straight:* immediately
     lay home to him: speak firmly with him
  2 *pranks:* mischievous tricks
     broad: unrestrained
 3–4   *your Grace ... him:* you have shielded him from criticism
  4 *I'll silence me:* I'll stop speaking
  5 *round:* outspoken
  7 *warrant:* assure, promise
     fear me not: do not worry about me
 10 *offended:* displeased, annoyed
 12 *with an idle tongue:* foolishly
 15 *by the rood:* by the cross of Christ
 18 *I'll set ... speak:* I'll get others to correct you
 19 *budge:* move, steal away
 20 *glass:* mirror
 21 *the inmost part of you:* what is deep inside you

Scene IV

The QUEEN'S *closet.*

Enter QUEEN *and* POLONIUS.

POLONIUS: He will come straight. Look you lay home to him.
   Tell him his pranks have been too broad to bear with,
   And that your Grace hath screened and stood between
   Much heat and him. I'll silence me e'en here.
5   Pray you be round with him.
HAMLET: *[Within]* Mother, mother, mother!
GERTRUDE: I'll warrant you; fear me not. Withdraw, I hear him
   coming.

POLONIUS *hides behind the arras.*

Enter HAMLET.

HAMLET: Now, mother, what's the matter?
10 **GERTRUDE:** Hamlet, thou hast thy father much offended.
HAMLET: Mother, you have my father much offended.
GERTRUDE: Come, come, you answer with an idle tongue.
HAMLET: Go, go, you question with a wicked tongue.
GERTRUDE: Why, how now, Hamlet?
HAMLET: What's the matter now?
15 **GERTRUDE:** Have you forgot me?
HAMLET: No, by the rood, not so!
   You are the queen, your husband's brother's wife,
   And, would it were not so, you are my mother.
GERTRUDE: Nay, then I'll set those to you that can speak.
HAMLET: Come, come, and sit you down, you shall not budge.
20   You go not till I set you up a glass
   Where you may see the inmost part of you.

25	*dead for a ducat:* I bet a ducat that I'll kill it
26	*slain:* killed
28	*rash:* overhasty
32	*intruding:* interfering
33	*thy better:* i.e. the king
34	*busy:* interfering, spying
35	*leave wringing:* stop squeezing
	peace: (exclamation) be quiet
37	*penetrable:* that allows sth. to be pushed into
38	*damnèd custom:* immoral habits
	brazed: hardened
39	*proof ... sense:* hardened against feeling
40–41	*dar'st ... rude:* dare to speak so rudely to me
42	*blurs:* stains
	grace and blush: innocence
43	*hypocrite:* pretender
45	*blister:* blemish; mark branded on a prostitute's forehead
46	*dicers' oaths:* gamblers' promises
47	*body of contraction:* marriage contract
47–48	*plucks the very soul:* tears the heart

GERTRUDE: What wilt thou do? Thou wilt not murder me?
Help, help, ho!
POLONIUS: *[Behind]* What, ho! Help, help, help!
25 **HAMLET:** *[Draws]* How now? A rat! Dead for a ducat, dead!

Makes a pass through the arras and kills POLONIUS.

POLONIUS: *[Behind]* O, I am slain!
GERTRUDE: O me, what hast thou done?
HAMLET: Nay, I know not. Is it the king?
GERTRUDE: O, what a rash and bloody deed is this!
HAMLET: A bloody deed? Almost as bad, good mother,
30 As kill a king, and marry with his brother.
GERTRUDE: As kill a king?
HAMLET: Ay, lady, it was my word.

Lifts up the arras and sees POLONIUS.

Thou wretched, rash, intruding fool, farewell.
I took thee for thy better. Take thy fortune.
Thou find'st to be too busy is some danger.
35 Leave wringing of your hands. Peace! Sit you down
And let me wring your heart, for so I shall
If it be made of penetrable stuff,
If damnèd custom have not brazed it so
That it is proof and bulwark against sense.
40 **GERTRUDE:** What have I done that thou dar'st wag thy tongue
In noise so rude against me?
HAMLET: Such an act
That blurs the grace and blush of modesty;
Calls virtue hypocrite; takes off the rose
From the fair forehead of an innocent love
45 And sets a blister there, makes marriage vows
As false as dicers' oaths. O, such a deed
As from the body of contraction plucks

49 *rhapsody:* meaningless jumble
  glow: blush for shame
50 *solidity and compound mass:* i.e. the world
51 *tristful visage:* sorrowful face
  the doom: doomsday, day of judgement
52 *thought-sick:* horror-struck
52 *index:* list of sins
55 *counterfeit presentment:* miniature portrait; likeness
57 *Hyperion; Jove:* the sun god; the king of gods
  front: forehead
58 *Mars:* god of war
59 *station:* posture, manner of standing
  herald Mercury: winged god of trade, Zeus's/Jove's messenger
60 *new-lighted:* just landed
  heaven-kissing: close to heaven
61–63 *combination ... man:* a figure and combination of good qualities as if every god had set his stamp on him
65 *mildewed ear:* rotten ear of corn (*Ähre*)
66 *blasting his wholesome brother:* infecting and killing his healthy brother
68 *batten:* feed greedily
  moor: swampy land
70 *heyday ... humble:* the wildness of youth and romantic passions are over
71 *waits upon the judgement:* i.e. the heart obeys reason
73 *motion:* emotions
74 *apoplexed:* not working properly
74–75 *for madness ... thralled:* nobody could be so insane that they could not choose this correctly
76–77 *but it ... difference:* but it could tell the difference
78 *cozened:* cheated, deceived
  hoodman-blind: children's game with blindfolds
80 *sans all:* without any of the other senses

The very soul, and sweet religion makes
A rhapsody of words! Heaven's face doth glow;
50 Yea, this solidity and compound mass,
With tristful visage, as against the doom,
Is thought-sick at the act.
GERTRUDE: Ay me, what act,
That roars so loud and thunders in the index?
HAMLET: Look here upon this picture, and on this,
55 The counterfeit presentment of two brothers.
See what a grace was seated on this brow;
Hyperion's curls, the front of Jove himself,
An eye like Mars, to threaten and command;
A station like the herald Mercury,
60 New-lighted on a heaven-kissing hill:
A combination and a form indeed
Where every god did seem to set his seal
To give the world assurance of a man.
This was your husband. Look you now what follows.
65 Here is your husband, like a mildewed ear
Blasting his wholesome brother. Have you eyes?
Could you on this fair mountain leave to feed,
And batten on this moor? Ha! Have you eyes?
You cannot call it love, for at your age
70 The heyday in the blood is tame, it's humble,
And waits upon the judgement; and what judgement
Would step from this to this? Sense sure you have,
Else could you not have motion; but sure that sense
Is apoplexed; for madness would not err,
75 Nor sense to ecstasy was ne'er so thralled
But it reserved some quantity of choice
To serve in such a difference. What devil was't
That thus hath cozened you at hoodman-blind?
Eyes without feeling, feeling without sight,
80 Ears without hands or eyes, smelling sans all,
Or but a sickly part of one true sense

82 *mope:* be stupid, unaware
84 *mutine in a matron's bones:* run riot in a married woman's body
85 *flaming:* burning
86 *proclaim:* publicly call it
87 *compulsive ardour gives the charge:* irresistible sexual passion of youth is
      overwhelming
88 *frost:* age
89 *panders will:* helps to satisfy sexual desire
91 *grainèd:* permanently embedded
92 *leave their tinct:* lose their colour
93 *enseamèd:* greasy; stained with semen
94 *stewed:* soaked
      honeying: exchanging endearments
95 *nasty sty:* filthy enclosure for pigs; brothel
98 *tithe:* tenth part
99 *precedent:* former
      vice: clown or trickster from Morality Plays
100 *cutpurse:* thief
101 *diadem:* crown
103 *shreds and patches:* rags and tatters; multicoloured costume of a fool on
      stage
105 *heavenly guards:* angels

Could not so mope.
O shame! Where is thy blush? Rebellious hell,
If thou canst mutine in a matron's bones,
85   To flaming youth let virtue be as wax
And melt in her own fire. Proclaim no shame
When the compulsive ardour gives the charge,
Since frost itself as actively doth burn,
And reason panders will.

GERTRUDE: O Hamlet, speak no more!
90   Thou turn'st mine eyes into my very soul,
And there I see such black and grainèd spots
As will not leave their tinct.

HAMLET: Nay, but to live
In the rank sweat of an enseamèd bed,
Stewed in corruption, honeying and making love
95   Over the nasty sty.

GERTRUDE: O, speak to me no more!
These words like daggers enter in mine ears.
No more, sweet Hamlet!

HAMLET: A murderer and a villain,
A slave that is not twentieth part the tithe
Of your precedent lord, a vice of kings,
100   A cutpurse of the empire and the rule,
That from a shelf the precious diadem stole
And put it in his pocket!

GERTRUDE: No more!

Enter the GHOST.

HAMLET: A king of shreds and patches –
Save me and hover o'er me with your wings,
105   You heavenly guards! – What would your gracious figure?

GERTRUDE: Alas, he's mad!

107 *tardy:* slow
    chide: criticize, scold, rebuke
108 *lapsed in time and passion:* strayed from his mission
    lets go by: delays
109 *th' important ... command:* the execution of your fear-inspiring order
110 *visitation:* visit
111 *whet ... purpose:* sharpen your weakened resolution
112 *amazement:* confusion
114 *conceit:* imagination
117 *bend your eye on:* look at
    vacancy: empty air
118 *incorporal:* empty
    hold discourse: speak
119 *forth ... peep:* you look very agitated
    spirits: vital spirits, a bodily liquid thought to be vital for life
121 *bedded hair:* smoothed down hair
    life in excrements: as if some tufts of hair had a life of their own
123 *distemper:* derangement
126 *his ... conjoined:* his appearance and the reason he has for appearing
127 *capable:* responsive
128 *lest:* in order to prevent sth. from happening
    piteous: inspiring pity
128–129 *convert my stern effects:* divert me from my firm intention to take revenge
130 *will want true colour:* will lack a real motive, will look wrong
    perchance: perhaps
137 *habit as he lived:* in his everyday clothes
138 *portal:* door

HAMLET: Do you not come your tardy son to chide,
　　That lapsed in time and passion lets go by
　　Th' important acting of your dread command? O, say!
110 **GHOST:** Do not forget. This visitation
　　Is but to whet thy almost blunted purpose.
　　But look, amazement on thy mother sits.
　　O, step between her and her fighting soul:
　　Conceit in weakest bodies strongest works.
115　　Speak to her, Hamlet.
　　HAMLET:　　　　　　　　How is it with you, lady?
　　GERTRUDE: Alas, how is't with you,
　　That you do bend your eye on vacancy,
　　And with th' incorporal air do hold discourse?
　　Forth at your eyes your spirits wildly peep;
120　　And, as the sleeping soldiers in th' alarm,
　　Your bedded hair, like life in excrements,
　　Start up and stand an end. O gentle son,
　　Upon the heat and flame of thy distemper
　　Sprinkle cool patience. Whereon do you look?
125 **HAMLET:** On him, on him! Look you how pale he glares.
　　His form and cause conjoined, preaching to stones,
　　Would make them capable. – Do not look upon me,
　　Lest with this piteous action you convert
　　My stern effects. Then what I have to do
130　　Will want true colour: tears perchance for blood.
　　GERTRUDE: To whom do you speak this?
　　HAMLET: Do you see nothing there?
　　GERTRUDE: Nothing at all; yet all that is I see.
　　HAMLET: Nor did you nothing hear?
135 **GERTRUDE:** No, nothing but ourselves.
　　HAMLET: Why, look you there! Look how it steals away!
　　My father, in his habit as he lived!
　　Look where he goes, even now out at the portal.

Exit GHOST.

139 *coinage:* creation, invention
140–141   *ecstasy is very cunning in:* which madness cleverly invents
142 *temperately:* calmly
143 *healthful:* healthy
144 *uttered:* spoken
   bring me to the test: try me
145 *reword:* say it differently
146 *gambol:* leap, jump
   love of grace: exclamation of impatience
147 *flattering unction:* appealing lotion
148 *trespass:* crime, offence
149 *skin and film the ulcerous place:* thinly cover a corrupted space
150 *mining all within:* undermining, working underground
152 *repent:* feel sorry for
154 *this my virtue:* my virtuous talk, i.e. in contrast to your vicious behaviour
155 *fatness:* vulgarity
   pursy: sick
157 *curb ... good:* bow and flatter for the chance to do good
158 *cleft my heart in twain:* split my heart in two
162 *assume a virtue:* pretend to be virtuous
163–164   *monster ... devil:* getting used to doing evil without feeling bad about it is easy
164 *is angel yet in this:* but there is one good thing about it
166 *frock or livery:* clothing or uniform
167 *aptly:* properly
   refrain: do not have sex with him
170 *for use ... nature:* habits can even change people's natural instinct
171 *curb:* control
172 *wondrous potency:* amazing power

GERTRUDE: This is the very coinage of your brain.
140   This bodiless creation ecstasy
       Is very cunning in.
     HAMLET: Ecstasy?
       My pulse as yours doth temperately keep time
       And makes as healthful music. It is not madness
       That I have uttered. Bring me to the test,
145   And I the matter will reword, which madness
       Would gambol from. Mother, for love of grace,
       Lay not that flattering unction to your soul,
       That not your trespass but my madness speaks.
       It will but skin and film the ulcerous place,
150   Whiles rank corruption, mining all within,
       Infects unseen. Confess yourself to heaven,
       Repent what's past; avoid what is to come,
       And do not spread the compost on the weeds
       To make them ranker. Forgive me this my virtue,
155   For in the fatness of these pursy times
       Virtue itself of vice must pardon beg,
       Yea, curb and woo for leave to do him good.
     GERTRUDE: O Hamlet, thou hast cleft my heart in twain.
     HAMLET: O, throw away the worser part of it,
160   And live the purer with the other half.
       Good night – but go not to my uncle's bed;
       Assume a virtue, if you have it not.
       That monster custom, who all sense doth eat,
       Of habits devil, is angel yet in this,
165   That to the use of actions fair and good
       He likewise gives a frock or livery
       That aptly is put on. Refrain tonight,
       And that shall lend a kind of easiness
       To the next abstinence, the next more easy,
170   For use almost can change the stamp of nature,
       And either curb the devil, or throw him out
       With wondrous potency. Once more, good night,

173 *are desirous to be blessed:* want to repent
174 *for this same lord:* i.e. for Polonius
175 *heaven hath pleased it so:* it is the divine will
177 *their scourge and minister:* heaven's executing officer
178 *bestow:* dispose of, get rid of
181 *remains behind:* lies ahead
183 *not ... do:* I beg you not to do this under any circumstances
184 *bloat:* flabby, swollen
185 *pinch wanton:* squeeze lustfully (so that she looks like a prostitute with make-up)
186 *reechy:* filthy
187 *paddling:* fingering amorously
188 *ravel ... out:* unravel, explain
190 *mad in craft:* pretending to be mad
190 *sober:* serious, earnest in judgement
192 *paddock:* toad (*Kröte*)
        gib: tomcat (*Kater*)
193 *dear concernings:* important matters
194 *in despite of sense and secrecy:* it is the better choice
195 *unpeg:* unfasten

Note, ll. 195–198: This is a reference to a lost story about a monkey with a basket of birds on a roof. The monkey imitated the birds flying out, fell and broke its neck.

197 *try conclusions:* experiment
200 *I have no life to breathe:* I am too exhausted to talk about what you said
202 *alack:* exclamation of sorrow
205 *adders fanged:* poisonous snakes

And when you are desirous to be blessed,
I'll blessing beg of you. For this same lord,
175 I do repent; but heaven hath pleased it so,
To punish me with this, and this with me,
That I must be their scourge and minister.
I will bestow him, and will answer well
The death I gave him. So again, good night.
180 I must be cruel, only to be kind;
Thus bad begins, and worse remains behind.
One word more, good lady.

GERTRUDE: What shall I do?

HAMLET: Not this, by no means, that I bid you do:
Let the bloat king tempt you again to bed,
185 Pinch wanton on your cheek, call you his mouse,
And let him, for a pair of reechy kisses,
Or paddling in your neck with his damned fingers,
Make you to ravel all this matter out,
That I essentially am not in madness,
190 But mad in craft. 'Twere good you let him know,
For who that's but a queen, fair, sober, wise,
Would from a paddock, from a bat, a gib
Such dear concernings hide? Who would do so?
No, in despite of sense and secrecy,
195 Unpeg the basket on the house's top,
Let the birds fly, and like the famous ape,
To try conclusions, in the basket creep
And break your own neck down.

GERTRUDE: Be thou assured, if words be made of breath,
200 And breath of life, I have no life to breathe
What thou hast said to me.

HAMLET: I must to England; you know that?

GERTRUDE: Alack,
I had forgot. 'Tis so concluded on.

HAMLET: There's letters sealed, and my two schoolfellows,
205 Whom I will trust as I will adders fanged,

206 *mandate:* orders

206–207 *sweep ... knavery:* lead my way to mischief

209 *hoist with his own petar:* blown up by his own bomb

210 *delve:* dig beneath

212 *in one ... meet:* two birds can be killed with one stone

213 *this man shall set me packing:* i.e. Polonius is the cause why I must leave at once

214 *lug the guts:* drag his body with effort

216 *secret, and most grave:* very quiet and dignified

217 *prating knave:* babbling idiot

218 *draw ... you:* haul you to your grave

   tugging in: pulling offstage

They bear the mandate. They must sweep my way
And marshal me to knavery. Let it work,
For 'tis the sport to have the engineer
Hoist with his own petar; an 't shall go hard
210 But I will delve one yard below their mines
And blow them at the moon. O, 'tis most sweet
When in one line two crafts directly meet.
This man shall set me packing.
I'll lug the guts into the neighbour room.
215 Mother, good night. Indeed, this counsellor
Is now most still, most secret, and most grave,
Who was in life a foolish prating knave.
Come, sir, to draw toward an end with you.
Good night, mother.

Exit the QUEEN.

Exit HAMLET, *tugging in* POLONIUS.

Summary:

Gertrude, still upset after her son's visit to her room, tells Claudius that Hamlet has stabbed Polonius through the tapestry without knowing who was hiding there. Claudius realises that he himself could have been the victim and does not comment on Polonius's fate at all. Calling Hamlet mad several times, Gertrude says that he is sorry for Polonius's death. Claudius assures her that he still loves his nephew, even though he is a threat to everyone. The king decides to exile Hamlet from Denmark immediately and orders Rosencrantz and Guildenstern to look for him and to take Polonius's body to the chapel. Trying to deal with this situation efficiently, Claudius wonders how to explain the murder to the public.

Annotations:

1 *profound:* heartfelt
   heaves: deep sighs
2 *translate:* explain
4 *bestow ... on us:* leave us
7 *contend:* fight
8 *lawless:* unruly
10 *rapier* [ˈreɪpɪə]: small sword
11 *brainish apprehension:* frantic state of mind
12 *heavy:* sorrowful
14 *liberty:* being unrestrained
16 *answered:* accounted for, explained
17 *providence:* foresight
18 *short:* confined, shut in
   out of haunt: out of the public

ACT IV

Scene I

Elsinore. A room in the castle.

Enter KING *and* QUEEN, *with* ROSENCRANTZ *and* GUILDENSTERN.

CLAUDIUS: There's matter in these sighs, these profound heaves.
    You must translate, 'tis fit we understand them.
    Where is your son?
GERTRUDE: Bestow this place on us a little while.

Exeunt ROSENCRANTZ *and* GUILDENSTERN.

5   Ah, mine own lord, what have I seen tonight!
CLAUDIUS: What, Gertrude? How does Hamlet?
GERTRUDE: Mad as the sea and wind when both contend
    Which is the mightier. In his lawless fit
    Behind the arras hearing something stir,
10   Whips out his rapier, cries 'A rat, a rat!'
    And in this brainish apprehension kills
    The unseen good old man.
CLAUDIUS: O heavy deed!
    It had been so with us, had we been there.
    His liberty is full of threats to all,
15   To you yourself, to us, to everyone.
    Alas, how shall this bloody deed be answered?
    It will be laid to us, whose providence
    Should have kept short, restrained, and out of haunt,
    This mad young man. But so much was our love,
20   We would not understand what was most fit,
    But like the owner of a foul disease,

22   *divulging:* becoming known
23   *pith:* essential part
24   *draw apart:* take aside
25–27   *ore … pure:* pure metal shows itself clearly among those of lesser quality
30   *hence:* away from here
32   *countenance* (v): make allowance for, confront
33   *go join … aid:* find others to help you
36   *fair:* pleasantly
40   *untimely:* wrongly
41   *discord and dismay:* conflicting feelings and fear

To keep it from divulging, let it feed
Even on the pith of life. Where is he gone?

GERTRUDE: To draw apart the body he hath killed;
25   O'er whom his very madness, like some ore
Among a mineral of metals base,
Shows itself pure; he weeps for what is done.

CLAUDIUS: O Gertrude, come away!
The sun no sooner shall the mountains touch
30   But we will ship him hence, and this vile deed
We must with all our majesty and skill
Both countenance and excuse. Ho, Guildenstern!

Enter ROSENCRANTZ *and* GUILDENSTERN.

Friends both, go join you with some further aid.
Hamlet in madness hath Polonius slain,
35   And from his mother's closet hath he dragged him.
Go seek him out, speak fair, and bring the body
Into the chapel. I pray you haste in this.

Exeunt ROSENCRANTZ *and* GUILDENSTERN.

Come, Gertrude, we'll call up our wisest friends
And let them know both what we mean to do
40   And what's untimely done. O, come away!
My soul is full of discord and dismay.

Exeunt.

Summary:

In a corridor of the castle, Rosencrantz and Guildenstern find Hamlet, who is speaking in riddles and does not tell them where Polonius's body is. The prince expresses his contempt for Rosencrantz, accusing him of being Claudius's bootlicker. Despite everything, Hamlet agrees to go with them to see the king.

Annotations:

1	*stowed:* disposed of, hidden
7	*compounded:* mixed
	kin: related
8	*thence:* from there
12	*keep your counsel:* keep your secrets
13	*sponge:* (here) one who seeks royal favour
	replication: reply
16	*countenance:* favour, patronage
17	*authorities:* influence; power
19	*mouthed:* put into the mouth
20	*gleaned:* gathered
23	*knavish:* sarcastic
	sleeps: goes unheard, is wasted

Scene II

Elsinore. A passage in the castle.

Enter HAMLET.

HAMLET: Safely stowed.
GENTLEMEN: *[Within]* Hamlet! Lord Hamlet!
HAMLET: But soft! What noise? Who calls on Hamlet? O, here they
    come.

Enter ROSENCRANTZ *and* GUILDENSTERN.

5   **ROSENCRANTZ:** What have you done, my lord, with the dead
        body?
    HAMLET: Compounded it with dust whereto 'tis kin.
    ROSENCRANTZ: Tell us where 'tis, that we may take it thence and
        bear it to the chapel.
10 **HAMLET:** Do not believe it.
    ROSENCRANTZ: Believe what?
    HAMLET: That I can keep your counsel, and not mine own.
        Besides, to be demanded of a sponge, what replication should
        be made by the son of a king?
15 **ROSENCRANTZ:** Take you me for a sponge, my lord?
    HAMLET: Ay, sir, that soaks up the king's countenance, his rewards,
        his authorities. But such officers do the king best service in the
        end: he keeps them like an ape in the corner of his jaw, first
        mouthed to be last swallowed. When he needs what you have
20   gleaned, it is but squeezing you and, sponge, you shall be dry
        again.
    ROSENCRANTZ: I understand you not, my lord.
    HAMLET: I am glad of it. A knavish speech sleeps in a foolish ear.
    ROSENCRANTZ: My lord, you must tell us where the body is, and
25   go with us to the king.

29   *hide fox:* reference to a game like hide-and-seek

HAMLET: The body is with the king, but the king is not with the
  body. The king is a thing –
GUILDENSTERN: A thing, my lord?
HAMLET: Of nothing. Bring me to him. Hide fox, and all after.

Exeunt.

Summary:

In the palace, Claudius explains to courtiers that Hamlet cannot remain in Elsinore because he is dangerous and, since Hamlet is much loved by the Danish people, Claudius cannot be as strict in his punishment as the case would demand it. His sending Hamlet away must therefore seem like a routine political undertaking. Rosencrantz and Guildenstern enter with Hamlet under guard. Hamlet is then asked about Polonius's whereabouts. Hamlet replies that the old man is feeding worms and uses allusions to death and decay by saying that worms do not even spare a king. Finally, Hamlet tells them that Polonius's body is beneath the stairs to the lobby. Claudius sends attendants to fetch the corpse and informs Hamlet that he must leave the country for his own protection, which the prince accepts without protest. To make sure that Hamlet gets on board the ship that departs for England, the king sends Rosencrantz and Guildenstern with him. They are to accompany Hamlet on the journey as well. When alone, Claudius reveals his plot to have Hamlet executed as soon as he arrives there. He has written letters containing his order to the English king, who cannot ignore his instruction because Claudius has had power over England since a Danish victory.

Annotations:

3 *strong law:* strict rules of law
4 *distracted multitude:* unreasonable general public
5 *like … eyes:* love him for his looks, not for good reasons
6 *scourge:* punishment
     weighed: considered
7 *bear … even:* manage all matters smoothly and evenly
9 *deliberate pause:* the result of thoughtful planning
10 *appliance:* solution, remedy
     relieved: helped
11 *befallen:* happened
12 *bestowed:* placed, hidden
14 *without:* outside
21 *convocation:* assembly
     politic: cunning, artful

Scene III

Elsinore. A room in the castle.

Enter KING.

CLAUDIUS: I have sent to seek him and to find the body.
How dangerous is it that this man goes loose.
Yet must not we put the strong law on him;
He's loved of the distracted multitude,
5   Who like not in their judgement, but their eyes;
And where 'tis so, th' offender's scourge is weighed,
But never the offence. To bear all smooth and even,
This sudden sending him away must seem
Deliberate pause. Diseases desperate grown
10   By desperate appliance are relieved,
Or not at all.

Enter ROSENCRANTZ.

How now? What hath befallen?
ROSENCRANTZ: Where the dead body is bestowed, my lord,
We cannot get from him.
CLAUDIUS: But where is he?
ROSENCRANTZ: Without, my lord, guarded, to know your pleasure.
15 **CLAUDIUS:** Bring him before us.
ROSENCRANTZ: Ho, Guildenstern! Bring in my lord.

Enter HAMLET *and* GUILDENSTERN *with* ATTENDANTS.

CLAUDIUS: Now, Hamlet, where's Polonius?
HAMLET: At supper.
CLAUDIUS: At supper? Where?
20 **HAMLET:** Not where he eats, but where he is eaten. A certain
convocation of politic worms are e'en at him. Your worm is your

22   *fat:* fatten
23   *maggots:* flesh-eating worms
       variable service: different dishes at a meal

Note, ll. 20–24: Hamlet's remarks about emperors, kings and beggars being
       ultimately food for worms echo the thought of French philosopher Michel
       de Montaigne (1533–1592): 'The heart and the life of a mighty emperor is
       but the breakfast of a worm.'

26   *eat:* eaten
29   *go a progress:* go on a journey
31   *thither:* to that place
33   *i' th' other place:* i.e. in hell
34   *nose* (v): smell
39   *do tender:* are concerned about, hold dear
41   *fiery:* fierce
42   *bark:* type of ship
43   *th' associates tend:* your company is ready for service
       bent: bound for, ready
46   *cherub:* angel

only emperor for diet: we fat all creatures else to fat us, and we
fat ourselves for maggots. Your fat king and your lean beggar is
but variable service, two dishes, but to one table, that's the end.

25 **CLAUDIUS:** Alas, alas.

HAMLET: A man may fish with the worm that hath eat of a king,
and eat of the fish that hath fed of that worm.

CLAUDIUS: What dost thou mean by this?

HAMLET: Nothing but to show you how a king may go a progress

30 through the guts of a beggar.

CLAUDIUS: Where is Polonius?

HAMLET: In heaven, send thither to see. If your messenger find
him not there, seek him i' th' other place yourself. But indeed, if
you find him not within this month, you shall nose him as you

35 go up the stairs into the lobby.

CLAUDIUS: *[To* ATTENDANTS.*]* Go seek him there.

HAMLET: He will stay till you come.

Exeunt ATTENDANTS.

CLAUDIUS: Hamlet, this deed, for thine especial safety,
Which we do tender, as we dearly grieve

40 For that which thou hast done, must send thee hence
With fiery quickness. Therefore prepare thyself.
The bark is ready and the wind at help,
Th' associates tend, and everything is bent
For England.

HAMLET: For England?

CLAUDIUS: Ay, Hamlet.

HAMLET: Good.

45 **CLAUDIUS:** So is it, if thou knew'st our purposes.

HAMLET: I see a cherub that sees them. But come, for England!
Farewell, dear mother.

CLAUDIUS: Thy loving father, Hamlet.

HAMLET: My mother. Father and mother is man and wife, man and

50 wife is one flesh, and so, my mother. Come, for England!

51	*at foot:* closely
	tempt him: make him go
54	*else leans on:* is connected with
55	*at aught:* to be worth anything
56	*sense:* reason to value
58–59	*cicatrice:* scar left by a wound
57	*thy ... us:* you pay tribute to us voluntarily
59	*coldly set:* ignore, disregard
60	*sovereign process:* royal command
	imports at full: gives detailed instructions
61	*congruing:* leading
62	*present:* immediate
63	*hectic:* fever
65	*haps:* fortunes

Exit.

CLAUDIUS: Follow him at foot; tempt him with speed aboard.
　　Delay it not, I'll have him hence tonight.
　　Away! For everything is sealed and done
　　That else leans on th' affair. Pray you make haste.

Exeunt ROSENCRANTZ *and* GUILDENSTERN.

55　And, England, if my love thou hold'st at aught,
　　As my great power thereof may give thee sense,
　　Since yet thy cicatrice looks raw and red
　　After the Danish sword, and thy free awe
　　Pays homage to us, thou mayst not coldly set
60　Our sovereign process, which imports at full,
　　By letters congruing to that effect,
　　The present death of Hamlet. Do it, England,
　　For like the hectic in my blood he rages,
　　And thou must cure me. Till I know 'tis done,
65　Howe'er my haps, my joys were ne'er begun.

Exit.

Summary:

Near the coast of Denmark, the Norwegian prince Fortinbras marches his army towards Poland and sends a captain to Elsinore Castle with the request for free passage through the country. When the captain meets Hamlet and his entourage, he tells him that the army will fight over a small stretch of land that is worthless. Hamlet tells Rosencrantz and Guildenstern to go ahead and is prompted to reflect on his own situation. Fortinbras and his 20,000 soldiers might die for honour, fighting for an unprofitable piece of soil. Hamlet doubts that he himself has acted honourably because he has delayed his revenge. However, being sent abroad, he has neither a plan, nor power, nor any resources to fulfil his duty at this point. He concludes, however, that honour must be defended and that from now on he will focus only on revenge.

Annotations:

  2   *licence:* permission
  3   *craves the conveyance:* desires an escort, asks for safe conduct
  4   *the rendezvous:* where to find him
  5   *would aught:* wishes to negotiate
  6   *duty:* respect
         in his eye: in his presence
  8   *softly:* carefully
  11 *how purposed:* with what purpose
  15 *the main:* the whole country
  17 *addition:* exaggeration
  22 *ranker rate:* better price
         in fee: directly

Scene IV

Near Elsinore.

Enter FORTINBRAS *with his* ARMY.

FORTINBRAS: Go, captain, from me greet the Danish king.
Tell him that by his licence, Fortinbras
Craves the conveyance of a promised march
Over his kingdom. You know the rendezvous.
5   If that his Majesty would aught with us,
We shall express our duty in his eye,
And let him know so.
CAPTAIN: I will do't, my lord.
FORTINBRAS: Go softly on.

Exeunt all but the CAPTAIN.

Enter HAMLET, ROSENCRANTZ, GUILDENSTERN, *and others.*

HAMLET: Good sir, whose powers are these?
10   **CAPTAIN:** They are of Norway, sir.
HAMLET: How purposed, sir, I pray you?
CAPTAIN: Against some part of Poland.
HAMLET: Who commands them, sir?
CAPTAIN: The nephew to old Norway, Fortinbras.
15   **HAMLET:** Goes it against the main of Poland, sir,
Or for some frontier?
CAPTAIN: Truly to speak, and with no addition,
We go to gain a little patch of ground
That hath in it no profit but the name.
20   To pay five ducats, five, I would not farm it,
Nor will it yield to Norway or the Pole
A ranker rate, should it be sold in fee.
HAMLET: Why, then the Polack never will defend it.

24 *garrisoned:* with troops put in place to defend it
26 *will ... straw:* cannot resolve this unimportant matter
27 *impostume:* abscess, inflammation
32 *occasions:* circumstances
   inform against: accuse
33 *spur* (v): hasten, drive
34 *chief good and market:* main profit
36 *he:* i.e. God
   discourse: intelligence
37 *before and after:* into the future and the past
39 *fust:* go stale
40 *bestial oblivion:* animal-like forgetfulness
   craven scruple: cowardly hesitation
41 *precisely:* scrupulously
42 *quartered:* cut into four pieces
45 *sith:* since
46 *gross as earth exhort me:* as heavy as earth urge me on
47 *mass and charge:* numbers and cost
49 *puffed:* inflated, made large
50 *makes ... event:* mocks death, puts his life at risk

CAPTAIN: Yes, it is already garrisoned.

25 **HAMLET:** Two thousand souls and twenty thousand ducats
Will not debate the question of this straw.
This is th' impostume of much wealth and peace,
That inward breaks, and shows no cause without
Why the man dies. I humbly thank you, sir.

30 **CAPTAIN:** God buy you, sir.

Exit.

ROSENCRANTZ: Will't please you go, my lord?
HAMLET: I'll be with you straight. Go a little before.

Exeunt all but HAMLET.

How all occasions do inform against me
And spur my dull revenge! What is a man,
If his chief good and market of his time
35 Be but to sleep and feed? A beast, no more.
Sure he that made us with such large discourse,
Looking before and after, gave us not
That capability and god-like reason
To fust in us unused. Now, whether it be
40 Bestial oblivion, or some craven scruple
Of thinking too precisely on th' event –
A thought which, quartered, hath but one part wisdom
And ever three parts coward – I do not know
Why yet I live to say 'This thing's to do',
45 Sith I have cause, and will, and strength, and means
To do't. Examples gross as earth exhort me.
Witness this army of such mass and charge,
Led by a delicate and tender prince,
Whose spirit, with divine ambition puffed,
50 Makes mouths at the invisible event,
Exposing what is mortal and unsure

57   *stained:* disgraced
58   *excitements:* provocations
         blood: passion
61   *fantasy and trick:* passing fancy and illusion
63   *whereon … cause:* which is too small to settle the matter
64   *continent:* container

To all that fortune, death, and danger dare,
Even for an eggshell. Rightly to be great
Is not to stir without great argument,
55 But greatly to find quarrel in a straw
When honour's at the stake. How stand I then,
That have a father killed, a mother stained,
Excitements of my reason and my blood,
And let all sleep, while to my shame I see
60 The imminent death of twenty thousand men,
That for a fantasy and trick of fame
Go to their graves like beds, fight for a plot
Whereon the numbers cannot try the cause,
Which is not tomb enough and continent
65 To hide the slain? O, from this time forth,
My thoughts be bloody, or be nothing worth.

Exit.

Summary:

In the palace, Gertrude is informed that Ophelia is in a disordered state of mind. Horatio warns the queen that not seeing Ophelia might have negative consequences for the royal family. Ophelia enters and sings distractedly of losses: of her father, of love and of losing one's virginity due to men's betrayal. Claudius arrives and, shocked to see Ophelia in this state, orders Horatio to follow and watch her closely once she leaves. The king worries a great deal about several problems: his cover-up of Hamlet's exile and Polonius's secret burial, Ophelia's apparent madness and Laertes's return from France. Laertes has also been influenced by troublemakers spreading rumours about his father's death. A messenger reports Elsinore to be in social unrest and that people claim Laertes should become king. Polonius's son suddenly bursts into the room and angrily demands to know the circumstances of his father's death, while Gertrude tries to defend Claudius. By calmly talking to Laertes, the king manages to pacify him and points out that he did not kill Polonius. Laertes is determined to seek bloodthirsty revenge and is deeply shocked at the sight of Ophelia. She has come in again, singing of death and handing out flowers and herbs to those who are present. Claudius promises Laertes to inform him of how Polonius died and why his death was hushed up. If the king is to blame, he will offer his crown to Laertes, whose revenge is fuelled even more after seeing his mad sister. Finally, Claudius assures Laertes that he will help him find justice.

Annotations:

  2 *importunate:* insistent
      distract (adj): mad
  3 *will needs be:* will have to be
      what would she have: what does she want
  5 *hems:* clears her throat
  6 *spurns ... straws:* gets angry at unimportant things
      in doubt: of unclear meaning
  9 *to collection:* to find a meaning in it
      aim: guess
 10 *botch:* piece together
 11 *which:* which words
      yield: convey
 12 *there ... thought:* she wants to convey a message
 14 *strew:* spread
 15 *conjectures:* ideas
      ill-breeding: trouble-making
 18 *toy:* unimportant thing
      amiss: misfortune
 19 *artless jealousy:* uncontrolled suspicion

Scene V

Elsinore. A room in the castle.

Enter HORATIO, QUEEN*, and a* GENTLEMAN.

GERTRUDE: I will not speak with her.
GENTLEMAN: She is importunate, indeed distract.
　Her mood will needs be pitied.
GERTRUDE:　　　　　　　　　What would she have?
GENTLEMAN: She speaks much of her father, says she hears
5　There's tricks i' th' world, and hems, and beats her heart,
　Spurns enviously at straws, speaks things in doubt,
　That carry but half sense. Her speech is nothing,
　Yet the unshapèd use of it doth move
　The hearers to collection. They aim at it,
10　And botch the words up fit to their own thoughts,
　Which, as her winks and nods and gestures yield them,
　Indeed would make one think there might be thought,
　Though nothing sure, yet much unhappily.
HORATIO: 'Twere good she were spoken with, for she may strew
15　Dangerous conjectures in ill-breeding minds.
GERTRUDE: Let her come in.

Exit GENTLEMAN.

　[Aside] To my sick soul, as sin's true nature is,
　Each toy seems prologue to some great amiss.
　So full of artless jealousy is guilt,
20　It spills itself in fearing to be spilt.

Enter OPHELIA *distracted.*

OPHELIA: Where is the beauteous Majesty of Denmark?
GERTRUDE: How now, Ophelia?

25 *cockle hat:* hat decorated with a shell emblem or shells
      staff: stick for walking
26 *shoon:* shoes

Note, ll. 25–26: Cockle hat, staff and sandals are items worn or used by pilgrims.
A scallop shell is the symbol of Saint James the Great.

27 *imports:* means
28 *mark:* pay attention
31 *turf:* piece of grassy land
36 *shroud:* death sheet
38 *larded:* decorated
40 *showers:* i.e. of flowers or tears
42 *good dild you:* may God reward you
45 *conceit:* thoughts
49 *betime:* early
52 *donned:* put on
53 *dupped:* unlocked, opened

OPHELIA: *[Sings]*
  How should I your true love know
  From another one?
25 *By his cockle hat and staff*
  And his sandal shoon.
GERTRUDE: Alas, sweet lady, what imports this song?
OPHELIA: Say you? Nay, pray you mark.
  [Sings] He is dead and gone, lady,
30 *He is dead and gone;*
  At his head a grass-green turf,
  At his heels a stone.
  Oho!
GERTRUDE: Nay, but Ophelia –
35 **OPHELIA:** Pray you mark.
  [Sings] White his shroud as the mountain snow –

Enter KING.

GERTRUDE: Alas, look here, my lord.
OPHELIA: *[Sings] Larded all with sweet flowers;*
  Which bewept to the grave did not go
40 *With true-love showers.*
CLAUDIUS: How do you, pretty lady?
OPHELIA: Well, good dild you. They say the owl was a baker's
  daughter. Lord, we know what we are, but know not what we
  may be. God be at your table!
45 **CLAUDIUS:** Conceit upon her father.
OPHELIA: Pray let's have no words of this, but when they ask you
  what it means, say you this.
  [Sings] Tomorrow is Saint Valentine's *day,*
  All in the morning betime,
50 *And I a maid at your window,*
  To be your Valentine.
  Then up he rose and donned his clothes
  And dupped the chamber door,

57 *without an oath:* I promise
58 *Gis:* Jesus
59 *alack and fie:* exclamations to express sorrow and dislike
61 *Cock:* God, but also word-play on *cock* = penis
62 *quoth:* said
    tumbled: had sex with
65 *yonder:* over there
66 *and:* if
71 *counsel:* advice
    coach: driver
76 *spies:* scouts sent ahead of an army
79 *remove:* removal
    muddied: confused
81 *greenly:* foolishly
82 *in hugger-mugger:* in secrecy
    inter [- '-]: bury

Let in the maid, that out a maid
55 *Never departed more.*
CLAUDIUS: Pretty Ophelia!
OPHELIA: Indeed, la, without an oath I'll make an end on't!
[Sings] By Gis and by Saint Charity,
Alack, and fie for shame!
60 *Young men will do't if they come to't.*
By Cock, they are to blame.
Quoth she, 'Before you tumbled me,
You promised me to wed.'
He answers:
65 *'So would I ha' done, by yonder sun,*
And thou hadst not come to my bed.'
CLAUDIUS: How long hath she been thus?
OPHELIA: I hope all will be well. We must be patient, but I cannot
choose but weep to think they would lay him i' th' cold ground.
70 My brother shall know of it, and so I thank you for your good
counsel. Come, my coach. Good night, ladies. Good night, sweet
ladies, good night, good night.

Exit.

CLAUDIUS: Follow her close; give her good watch, I pray you.

Exit HORATIO.

O, this is the poison of deep grief, it springs
75 All from her father's death. O Gertrude, Gertrude,
When sorrows come, they come not single spies,
But in battalions. First, her father slain;
Next, your son gone, and he most violent author
Of his own just remove; the people muddied,
80 Thick and unwholesome in their thoughts and whispers
For good Polonius' death – and we have done but greenly
In hugger-mugger to inter him; poor Ophelia

84 *pictures:* images
87 *feeds ... clouds:* images all sorts of things
88 *wants not buzzers:* is surrounded by gossip-mongers
89 *pestilent speeches:* wicked stories
90 *wherein ... beggared:* lacking facts and evidence
91 *will nothing stick:* will stop at nothing
91–92 *arraign in ear and ear:* accuse publicly
93 *murdering piece:* small cannon
94 *superfluous death:* multiple deaths
96 *attend:* (exclamation) attention
    Switzers: Swiss guards
99 *overpeering of his list:* rising above its boundary
100 *flats:* low land near the shore
    impetuous: pitiless
101 *head:* advance party (*Vorhut*)
102 *o'erbears:* overwhelms
    rabble: violent mob
103 *and:* as if
104 *antiquity:* ancient times, especially Greek and Roman times
    custom: traditional values and conventions
105 *ratifiers and props:* supporters

Divided from herself and her fair judgement,
Without the which we are pictures, or mere beasts;
85 Last, and as much containing as all these,
Her brother is in secret come from France,
Feeds on his wonder, keeps himself in clouds,
And wants not buzzers to infect his ear
With pestilent speeches of his father's death,
90 Wherein necessity, of matter beggared,
Will nothing stick our person to arraign
In ear and ear. O my dear Gertrude, this,
Like to a murdering piece, in many places
Gives me superfluous death.

A noise within.

95 **GERTRUDE:** Alack, what noise is this?
CLAUDIUS: Attend! Where are my Switzers? Let them guard the
door.

Enter a MESSENGER.

What is the matter?
MESSENGER: Save yourself, my lord:
The ocean, overpeering of his list,
100 Eats not the flats with more impetuous haste
Than young Laertes, in a riotous head,
O'erbears your offices. The rabble call him lord,
And, as the world were now but to begin,
Antiquity forgot, custom not known,
105 The ratifiers and props of every word,
They cry 'Choose we! Laertes shall be king!'
Caps, hands and tongues applaud it to the clouds,
'Laertes shall be king! Laertes king!'

A noise within.

110 *counter:* wrong-headed
     false: disloyal
116 *keep:* guard
118 *proclaims me bastard:* calls me not rightful (because my father is not
     revenged yet)
119 *cuckold:* deceived husband
     brands the harlot: marks the prostitute by burning
120 *between:* in the middle of
     chaste unsmirchèd: pure and unsoiled
121 *true:* faithful
123 *fear:* fear for
124 *divinity:* quality of being like a god
     hedge: surround; protect
125 *peep to what it would:* look quickly at what it desires
126 *acts little of his will:* cannot do what it wants to
127 *incensed:* very angry
129 *demand his fill:* ask everything he wants to know
130 *be juggled with:* have tricks played on me
131 *allegiance:* loyalty
     vows: promises of loyalty

GERTRUDE: How cheerfully on the false trail they cry!
110   O, this is counter, you false Danish dogs!
CLAUDIUS: The doors are broke.

Enter LAERTES *with others.*

LAERTES: Where is this king? Sirs, stand you all without.
ALL: No, let's come in!
LAERTES: I pray you give me leave.
115 **ALL:** We will, we will.
LAERTES: I thank you. Keep the door.

Exeunt his FOLLOWERS.

                                    O thou vile king,
    Give me my father!
GERTRUDE: Calmly, good Laertes.
LAERTES: That drop of blood that's calm proclaims me bastard;
    Cries cuckold to my father, brands the harlot
120   Even here, between the chaste unsmirchèd brow
    Of my true mother.
CLAUDIUS: What is the cause, Laertes,
    That thy rebellion looks so giant-like?
    Let him go, Gertrude, do not fear our person.
    There's such divinity doth hedge a king
125   That treason can but peep to what it would,
    Acts little of his will. –Tell me, Laertes,
    Why thou art thus incensed. Let him go, Gertrude.
    – Speak, man.
LAERTES: Where is my father?
CLAUDIUS: Dead.
GERTRUDE: But not by him.
CLAUDIUS: Let him demand his fill.
130 **LAERTES:** How came he dead? I'll not be juggled with:
    To hell allegiance, vows to the blackest devil,

133 *I dare damnation:* I disregard everlasting torment in hell
       to this point I stand: this is what I believe
134 *both … negligence:* I care neither for heaven nor hell
136 *throughly:* thoroughly
       stay: stop, prevent
138 *husband:* manage
141 *is't writ:* is it written
142 *swoopstake:* i.e. as in a lottery
       draw: gather
       foe: enemy
145 *ope:* open
146 *life-rendering:* life-giving
147 *repast:* feed

Note, ll. 146–147: It was believed that the pelican would cut its own breast
open with its beak and feed its young with its blood if food was scarce.

150 *most sensibly:* with strong feelings
151 *level:* well-aimed, directly
       pierce: go through sharply
154 *salt:* saltier
155 *sense and virtue:* power and effectiveness

Conscience and grace to the profoundest pit!
I dare damnation. To this point I stand,
That both the worlds I give to negligence,
135 Let come what comes, only I'll be revenged
Most throughly for my father.
CLAUDIUS: Who shall stay you?
LAERTES: My will, not all the world!
And for my means, I'll husband them so well,
They shall go far with little.
CLAUDIUS: Good Laertes,
140 If you desire to know the certainty
Of your dear father's death, is't writ in your revenge
That, swoopstake, you will draw both friend and foe,
Winner and loser?
LAERTES: None but his enemies.
CLAUDIUS: Will you know them then?
145 **LAERTES:** To his good friends thus wide I'll ope my arms,
And, like the kind life-rendering pelican,
Repast them with my blood.
CLAUDIUS: Why, now you speak
Like a good child and a true gentleman.
That I am guiltless of your father's death,
150 And am most sensibly in grief for it,
It shall as level to your judgement pierce
As day does to your eye.

A noise within: 'Let her come in.'

LAERTES: How now, what noise is that?

Enter OPHELIA.

O heat, dry up my brains, tears seven times salt
155 Burn out the sense and virtue of mine eye!
By heaven, thy madness shall be paid with weight

157 *our scale turn the beam:* bis die Waagschale sich zu unseren Gunsten senkt
161 *nature:* human nature
　　fine in: refined by
162 *instance:* part
163 *thing:* i.e. Polonius
164 *bier:* frame on which a coffin is placed before burial
168 *persuade:* argue for
170–171 *You must sing … a-down-a:* i.e. the bystanders are to sing a refrain
171 *wheel:* refrain; change in rhythm
171–172 *false steward … daughter:* reference to a lost song
173 *this … matter:* this nonsense says more than words could do
175 *pansies: Stiefmütterchen*
176 *document:* lesson
　　thoughts: melancholy
177 *fitted:* put together
178 *fennel:* herb symbolizing flattery; *Fenchelblüte*
　　columbines: flowers symbolizing faithlessness or ingratitude; *Akelei*
　　rue: plant symbolizing regret or repentance; *Weinlaub*
178 *herb of grace o' Sundays:* i.e. a herb belonging to the saying of prayers in church on Sundays
180 *with a difference:* differently
181 *daisy:* flower symbolizing unrequited love or deception; *Gänseblümchen*
　　violets: flowers symbolizing purity and faithfulness; *Veilchen*
　　withered: dried, faded
184 *passion:* grief, suffering
185 *favour:* charm

Till our scale turn the beam. O rose of May!
Dear maid, kind sister, sweet Ophelia!
O heavens, is't possible a young maid's wits
160 Should be as mortal as an old man's life?
Nature is fine in love, and where 'tis fine,
It sends some precious instance of itself
After the thing it loves.

OPHELIA: *[Sings]*
They bore him bare-faced on the bier,
165 *Hey non nonny, nonny, hey nonny,*
And in his grave rained many a tear –
Fare you well, my dove!

LAERTES: Hadst thou thy wits, and didst persuade revenge,
It could not move thus.

170 **OPHELIA:** You must sing *A-down a-down*, and you *Call him a-down-
a*. O, how the wheel becomes it! It is the false steward that stole
his master's daughter.

LAERTES: This nothing's more than matter.

OPHELIA: There's rosemary, that's for remembrance. Pray you, love,
175 remember. And there is pansies, that's for thoughts.

LAERTES: A document in madness, thoughts and remembrance
fitted.

OPHELIA: There's fennel for you, and columbines. There's rue for
you, and here's some for me; we may call it herb of grace o'
180 Sundays. O, you must wear your rue with a difference. There's a
daisy. I would give you some violets, but they withered all when
my father died. They say he made a good end.
[Sings] For bonny sweet Robin is all my joy.

LAERTES: Thought and affliction, passion, hell itself,
185 She turns to favour and to prettiness.

OPHELIA: *[Sings]*
And will he not come again?
And will he not come again?
No, no, he is dead,
Go to thy death-bed,

192   *all flaxen was his poll:* his hair was white
194   *cast away moan:* grieve uselessly
198   *commune with:* share
199   *go but apart:* go where you want
200   *of whom:* whichever of
201   *'twixt:* between
202   *collateral:* indirect
203   *touched:* involved, guilty
206   *lend:* grant, give
207   *labour* (v): work
208   *due content:* the satisfaction it deserves
209   *obscure:* not done with the proper funeral rites
210   *trophy:* memorial
          hatchment: tomb bearing the coat of arms
211   *ostentation:* solemn ceremony
213   *that:* so that
          call't in question: demand an explanation

190   *He never will come again.*
       His beard was as white as snow,
       All flaxen was his poll.
       He is gone, he is gone,
       And we cast away moan.
195   *God-a-mercy on his soul.*
       And of all Christian souls, I pray God. God buy you.

Exit.

LAERTES: Do you see this, O God?
CLAUDIUS: Laertes, I must commune with your grief,
       Or you deny me right. Go but apart,
200   Make choice of whom your wisest friends you will,
       And they shall hear and judge 'twixt you and me.
       If by direct or by collateral hand
       They find us touched, we will our kingdom give,
       Our crown, our life, and all that we call ours,
205   To you in satisfaction. But if not,
       Be you content to lend your patience to us,
       And we shall jointly labour with your soul
       To give it due content.
LAERTES: Let this be so.
       His means of death, his obscure funeral,
210   No trophy, sword, nor hatchment o'er his bones,
       No noble rite nor formal ostentation,
       Cry to be heard, as 'twere from heaven to earth,
       That I must call't in question.
CLAUDIUS: So you shall.
       And where th' offence is let the great axe fall.
215   I pray you go with me.

Exeunt.

Summary:

Sailors arrive to deliver a letter to Horatio, who has stayed in Elsinore after Hamlet's departure. He learns that Hamlet's ship was attacked by pirates in a sea battle and that the prince was captured. Rosencrantz and Guildenstern are still on their way to England. Being in Denmark after having made a deal with the pirates, Hamlet sends a letter to Claudius and asks Horatio to meet him as soon as possible. Horatio asks the sailors to take him to Hamlet at once.

Annotations:

  8 *and please him:* if it pleases him

Note, l. 9: The sailor's reference to the 'ambassador' may indicate that Hamlet concealed his true identity from the sailors.

12 *some means:* the opportunity to approach
     ere: before
13 *pirate:* pirate ship
     of very warlike appointment: heavily armed
13–14 *gave us chase:* followed us seeking conflict
14–15 *put on a compelled valour:* had to be courageous
15 *grapple:* close fight
17 *thieves of mercy:* compassionate thieves
19 *repair:* come
20 *fly:* flee
     make thee dumb: silence you
21 *the bore of the matter:* the importance of their meaning

Note, ll. 21: The metaphor Hamlet uses is that of a shot that is too small ('much too light') for the bore (*Kaliber*) of the cannon.

Scene VI

Elsinore. Another room in the castle.

Enter HORATIO *with a* SERVANT.

HORATIO: What are they that would speak with me?
SERVANT: Seafaring men, sir. They say they have letters for you.
HORATIO: Let them come in.

Exit SERVANT.

I do not know from what part of the world
5   I should be greeted, if not from Lord Hamlet.

Enter SAILORS.

SAILOR: God bless you, sir.
HORATIO: Let him bless thee too.
SAILOR: 'A shall, sir, and please him. There's a letter for you, sir, it
came from th' ambassador that was bound for England, if your
10   name be Horatio, as I am let to know it is.
HORATIO: *[Reads the letter]*
Horatio, when thou shalt have overlooked this, give these fellows
some means to the king, they have letters for him. Ere we were
two days old at sea, a pirate of very warlike appointment gave us
chase. Finding ourselves too slow of sail, we put on a compelled
15   *valour, and in the grapple I boarded them. On the instant they*
got clear of our ship, so I alone became their prisoner. They have
dealt with me like thieves of mercy, but they knew what they did: I
am to do a good turn for them. Let the king have the letters I have
sent, and repair thou to me with as much speed as thou wouldst
20   *fly death. I have words to speak in thine ear will make thee dumb,*
yet are they much too light for the bore of the matter. These good
fellows will bring thee where I am. Rosencrantz and Guildenstern

28   *speedier:* faster

hold their course for England. Of them I have much to tell thee.
Farewell.

25   *He that thou knowest thine,*
                                      Hamlet.

Come, I will give you way for these your letters,
And do't the speedier that you may direct me
To him from whom you brought them.

Exeunt.

Summary:

Alone with Laertes, Claudius explains that Hamlet mistakenly stabbed Polonius thinking it was the king (who he actually wanted to kill). His two reasons to conceal the crime were that Hamlet is much loved by the public and his mother, and that Claudius loves Gertrude dearly and did not want to cause her distress. After reading Hamlet's letter brought in by a messenger, Claudius is shocked at the news of his nephew's imminent return and immediately suggests a plan on how Laertes could avenge Polonius while making it look like an accident – even to Gertrude. Claudius thinks that Hamlet would not be able to resist a fencing match against Laertes to test his own skills, and his plan is, against all rules, to keep one foil sharp at the tip. It is Laertes's idea to bait this tip with poison so that even a small scratch can kill Hamlet. As a backup plan, Claudius intends to poison a drink he will offer Hamlet for refreshment. When Gertrude enters and tells how Ophelia has fallen from a tree into a river and drowned, Laertes is unable to hide his tears and leaves, grief-stricken. Claudius worries that Laertes's rage might be inflamed again.

Annotations:

1 *conscience my acquittance seal:* judgement confirm my innocence
3 *sith:* since
     knowing: understanding
6 *feats:* actions
7 *crimeful:* criminal
     capital: deserving a death sentence
8 *as … else:* given that it was in the interest of safety and carefulness
9 *mainly:* greatly
     stirred up: concerned, disturbed
10 *unsinewed:* weak
13 *plague:* torment
14 *conjunctive:* closely united with
16 *could not but by her:* cannot live or move without her
17 *count:* account, reckoning
18 *gender:* population
19 *dipping:* ignoring
20 *spring … stone:* water with much lime (*Kalk*) in it turns wood to stone
21 *gyves:* chains; (here) deformities, misdeeds
22 *too slightly timbered:* not strong enough
23 *reverted:* returned, come back
26 *desperate terms:* hopeless circumstances
27 *if … again:* if praise may remember her as she was

Scene VII

Elsinore. Another room in the castle.

Enter KING *and* LAERTES.

CLAUDIUS: Now must your conscience my acquittance seal,
    And you must put me in your heart for friend,
    Sith you have heard, and with a knowing ear,
    That he which hath your noble father slain
5   Pursued my life.
    LAERTES: It well appears. But tell me
    Why you proceeded not against these feats
    So crimeful and so capital in nature,
    As by your safety, wisdom, all things else
    You mainly were stirred up.
    CLAUDIUS: O, for two special reasons,
10   Which may to you, perhaps, seem much unsinewed,
    But yet to me they're strong. The queen his mother
    Lives almost by his looks, and for myself,
    My virtue or my plague, be it either which,
    She's so conjunctive to my life and soul,
15   That as the star moves not but in his sphere,
    I could not but by her. The other motive,
    Why to a public count I might not go,
    Is the great love the general gender bear him,
    Who, dipping all his faults in their affection,
20   Work like the spring that turneth wood to stone,
    Convert his gyves to graces, so that my arrows,
    Too slightly timbered for so loud a wind,
    Would have reverted to my bow again,
    And not where I had aimed them.
25 **LAERTES:** And so have I a noble father lost;
    A sister driven into desperate terms,
    Whose worth, if praises may go back again,

28–29   *stood ... perfections:* was the most perfect of all women
31   *flat:* unfeeling
33   *pastime* (adj): unimportant
43   *naked:* without the necessary things for life
45   *pardon:* permission
          recount: tell in detail
49   *abuse:* deception; trick
          no such thing: nothing like that has happened
50   *hand:* handwriting
          character: style or handwriting
53   *devise:* advise, help

Stood challenger on mount of all the age
For her perfections. But my revenge will come.

30 **CLAUDIUS:** Break not your sleeps for that. You must not think
That we are made of stuff so flat and dull
That we can let our beard be shook with danger
And think it pastime. You shortly shall hear more.
I loved your father, and we love ourself,

35 And that, I hope, will teach you to imagine –

Enter a MESSENGER *with letters.*

How now? What news?
MESSENGER: Letters, my lord, from Hamlet:
This to your Majesty, this to the queen.
CLAUDIUS: From Hamlet? Who brought them?
MESSENGER: Sailors, my lord, they say, I saw them not.

40 They were given me by Claudio – he received them
Of him that brought them.
CLAUDIUS: Laertes, you shall hear them.
Leave us.

Exit MESSENGER.

*[Reads] High and Mighty, you shall know I am set naked on your
kingdom. Tomorrow shall I beg leave to see your kingly eyes, when*

45 *I shall, first asking your pardon thereunto, recount th' occasion of
my sudden and more strange return.*

                                        Hamlet.

What should this mean? Are all the rest come back?
Or is it some abuse, and no such thing?

50 **LAERTES:** Know you the hand?
CLAUDIUS: 'Tis Hamlet's character.
'Naked' –
And in a postscript here, he says 'alone'.
Can you devise me?

55 *warms:* inflames
57 *thus didest thou:* this is what you did
60 *o'errule me to a peace:* lead me toward peace
62 *as checking at:* not continuing
63 *work:* persuade
64 *exploit:* plot, undertaking
   ripe in my device: which I have thought out
65 *shall not choose but:* has to
67 *uncharge the practice:* make excuses for the trick
69 *the rather:* the better
   devise: arrange
70 *the organ:* the one who does the deed
   falls right: falls into place, turns out right
73 *parts:* abilities, accomplishments
74 *pluck:* inspire, cause
76 *unworthiest siege:* far from your best attribute
77 *riband:* ribbon for decoration
78 *needful:* necessary
79 *livery:* clothes
80 *sables:* dark clothes
   weeds: dignified garments
81 *importing:* signifying
   graveness: dignity

LAERTES: I am lost in it, my lord. But let him come.
55   It warms the very sickness in my heart
      That I shall live and tell him to his teeth
      'Thus didest thou.'
CLAUDIUS: If it be so, Laertes –
      As how should it be so, how otherwise? –
      Will you be ruled by me?
LAERTES: Ay my lord,
60   So you will not o'errule me to a peace.
CLAUDIUS: To thine own peace. If he be now returned,
      As checking at his voyage, and that he means
      No more to undertake it, I will work him
      To an exploit, now ripe in my device,
65   Under the which he shall not choose but fall,
      And for his death no wind shall breathe,
      But even his mother shall uncharge the practice
      And call it accident.
LAERTES: My lord, I will be ruled,
      The rather if you could devise it so
70   That I might be the organ.
CLAUDIUS: It falls right.
      You have been talked of since your travel much,
      And that in Hamlet's hearing, for a quality
      Wherein they say you shine. Your sum of parts
      Did not together pluck such envy from him
75   As did that one, and that in my regard
      Of the unworthiest siege.
LAERTES: What part is that, my lord?
CLAUDIUS: A very riband in the cap of youth,
      Yet needful too, for youth no less becomes
      The light and careless livery that it wears
80   Than settled age his sables and his weeds,
      Importing health and graveness. Two months since
      Here was a gentleman of Normandy.
      I have seen myself, and served against, the French,

84 *can well:* are very skilled
    gallant (n): fine young man
86 *wondrous:* admirable
87 *as:* as if
    encorpsed and demi-natured: half grown together with his horse
88 *topped my thought:* surpassed my imagination
89–90 *that I ... he did:* that he performed tricks and movements that I could
    never have imagined
90 *Norman:* from Normandy
93 *brooch:* piece of jewelry; (here) the best of all
94 *gem:* precious stone
95 *made confession of you:* said he knew you
97 *art ... defence:* expertise in swordplay
98 *rapier* [ˈreɪpɪə]: small sword
    especial: especially
100 *th'escrimers:* experts on fencing
101 *guard:* defence
103 *envenom* (v): poison
105 *sudden:* immediate
    play: compete in a fencing match
108 *painting:* image
111 *begun by time:* generated in certain circumstances
112 *passages of proof:* events that proved it
113 *qualifies:* dulls, weakens

And they can well on horseback, but this gallant
85   Had witchcraft in't. He grew unto his seat,
And to such wondrous doing brought his horse
As had he been incorpsed and demi-natured
With the brave beast. So far he topped my thought,
That I in forgery of shapes and tricks
90   Come short of what he did.

LAERTES: A Norman was't?

CLAUDIUS: A Norman.

LAERTES: Upon my life, Lamord.

CLAUDIUS: The very same.

LAERTES: I know him well, he is the brooch indeed
And gem of all the nation.

95 **CLAUDIUS:** He made confession of you,
And gave you such a masterly report
For art and exercise in your defence,
And for your rapier most especial,
That he cried out 'twould be a sight indeed
100   If one could match you. Th' escrimers of their nation
He swore had neither motion, guard, nor eye,
If you opposed them. Sir, this report of his
Did Hamlet so envenom with his envy
That he could nothing do but wish and beg
105   Your sudden coming o'er to play with you.
Now, out of this –

LAERTES: What out of this, my lord?

CLAUDIUS: Laertes, was your father dear to you?
Or are you like the painting of a sorrow,
A face without a heart?

LAERTES: Why ask you this?

110 **CLAUDIUS:** Not that I think you did not love your father,
But that I know love is begun by time,
And that I see, in passages of proof,
Time qualifies the spark and fire of it.
There lives within the very flame of love

115 *wick:* cord in a candle
snuff: burning wick
abate: extinguish; put out
116 *is at a like goodness still:* remains good forever
117 *plurisy:* excess, overabundance
118 *would:* want to
120 *abatements:* decline; fading
122 *spendthrift:* wasteful, extravagant
123 *easing:* relief
quick of th'ulcer: heart of the matter
127 *sanctuarize:* protect
128 *bounds:* limits
129 *keep close:* stay inside
132 *set a double varnish on the fame:* praise you even more than
133 *in fine:* finally
134 *wager:* bet on the outcome
remiss: unsuspecting
135 *generous:* noble-minded
contriving: deceitful behaviour
136 *peruse the foils:* carefully examine the light swords
137 *unbated:* with a sharp tip
pass of practice: push or stroke with the foil
139 *requite:* repay
140 *anoint:* put on a liquid
141 *unction:* ointment, poison
mountebank: quack doctor
142 *cataplasm:* countermeasure, antidote
rare: excellent
144 *simples:* herbs used for medicine
146 *withal:* with it

115 A kind of wick or snuff that will abate it,
And nothing is at a like goodness still,
For goodness, growing to a plurisy,
Dies in his own too much. That we would do,
We should do when we would, for this 'would' changes,
120 And hath abatements and delays as many
As there are tongues, are hands, are accidents;
And then this 'should' is like a spendthrift sigh,
That hurts by easing. But to the quick of th' ulcer –
Hamlet comes back. What would you undertake
125 To show yourself your father's son in deed
More than in words?
  LAERTES: To cut his throat i' th' church.
  CLAUDIUS: No place indeed should murder sanctuarize;
Revenge should have no bounds. But, good Laertes,
Will you do this, keep close within your chamber;
130 Hamlet, returned, shall know you are come home.
We'll put on those shall praise your excellence
And set a double varnish on the fame
The Frenchman gave you; bring you in fine together,
And wager on your heads. He, being remiss,
135 Most generous, and free from all contriving,
Will not peruse the foils, so that with ease,
Or with a little shuffling, you may choose
A sword unbated, and, in a pass of practice
Requite him for your father.
  LAERTES: I will do't.
140 And for that purpose I'll anoint my sword.
I bought an unction of a mountebank,
So mortal that but dip a knife in it,
Where it draws blood no cataplasm so rare,
Collected from all simples that have virtue
145 Under the moon, can save the thing from death
This is but scratched withal. I'll touch my point

147 *contagion:* poison
     gall: hurt by touching
149 *weigh:* consider
150 *shape:* plan
151 *drift:* aim; scheme
152 *assayed:* tried
153 *back or second:* backup plan
154 *blast in proof:* fail
155 *solemn:* earnest
     cunnings: skills
156 *I ha't:* I have it
158 *as make your bouts:* you should make your rounds
159 *and that:* in case
     preferred: prepared
160 *chalice:* cup
     nonce: occasion, purpose
161 *venomed stuck:* poisoned thrust
162 *purpose may hold there:* plan will be successful
164 *woe:* sorrow, heartbreak
167 *willow:* type of tree; *Trauerweide*
     askant: leaning over
     brook: small river
168 *hoar* (adj): grey, whitish
169 *fantastic:* fanciful
170 *crow-flowers:* type of flowers; *Ranunkeln*
     nettles: type of plant; *Nesseln*
     purples: type of flowers; *lila Orchideen*
171 *liberal:* freely spoken
     grosser: more vulgar (because the roots of orchids resemble testicles)
172 *cold:* chaste, pure
173 *pendant boughs:* hanging branches
     coronet weeds: weeds/flowers made into a wreath
174 *clamb'ring to:* climbing in order to
     envious sliver: malicious branch
175 *weedy:* made of wild flowers

With this contagion, that if I gall him slightly,
It may be death.
CLAUDIUS: Let's further think of this,
Weigh what convenience both of time and means
150   May fit us to our shape. If this should fall,
And that our drift look through our bad performance,
'Twere better not assayed. Therefore this project
Should have a back or second, that might hold
If this did blast in proof. Soft, let me see.
155   We'll make a solemn wager on your cunnings –
I ha't!
When in your motion you are hot and dry,
As make your bouts more violent to that end,
And that he calls for drink, I'll have preferred him
160   A chalice for the nonce, whereon but sipping,
If he by chance escape your venomed stuck,
Our purpose may hold there. But stay, what noise?

Enter QUEEN.

How now, sweet queen?
GERTRUDE: One woe doth tread upon another's heel,
165   So fast they follow. Your sister's drowned, Laertes.
LAERTES: Drowned! O, where?
GERTRUDE: There is a willow grows askant a brook,
That shows his hoar leaves in the glassy stream.
There with fantastic garlands did she make
170   Of crow-flowers, nettles, daisies, and long purples,
That liberal shepherds give a grosser name,
But our cold maids do dead men's fingers call them.
There on the pendant boughs her coronet weeds
Clamb'ring to hang, an envious sliver broke,
175   When down her weedy trophies and herself
Fell in the weeping brook. Her clothes spread wide
And mermaid-like awhile they bore her up,

178   *which time:* at which time
        chanted: sang
        snatches of old lauds: parts of old hymns
179   *incapable of:* not aware of
        distress: calamity, dangerous situation
180   *native and indued unto:* born in and adapted to
183   *lay:* song
188   *trick:* way
        nature her custom holds: we do what is in our nature
189   *these:* i.e. his tears
190   *the woman will be out:* I will have finished behaving like a woman
191   *I have … blaze:* I could speak some fiery words
192   *this folly douts it:* my foolish tears drown them out

Which time she chanted snatches of old lauds
As one incapable of her own distress,
180 Or like a creature native and indued
Unto that element. But long it could not be
Till that her garments, heavy with their drink,
Pulled the poor wretch from her melodious lay
To muddy death.

LAERTES: Alas, then she is drowned?

185 **GERTRUDE:** Drowned, drowned.

LAERTES: Too much of water hast thou, poor Ophelia,
And therefore I forbid my tears. But yet
It is our trick; nature her custom holds,
Let shame say what it will. When these are gone,
190 The woman will be out. Adieu, my lord.
I have a speech of fire, that fain would blaze
But that this folly douts it.

Exit.

CLAUDIUS: Let's follow, Gertrude.
How much I had to do to calm his rage!
Now fear I this will give it start again.
195 Therefore let's follow.

Exeunt.

Summary:

In a churchyard, two gravediggers are preparing Ophelia's grave. Since her death could be seen as a suicide, they discuss whether she deserves a Christian burial. As Hamlet and Horatio come along, one gravedigger throws up two skulls out of the grave and tells Hamlet that one of them belonged to Yorick, the court's jester. Holding the skull in his hand, Hamlet reflects about mortality. When the funeral procession approaches, Hamlet realises that it is Ophelia's burial. Laertes, frantic with grief, leaps into the grave, followed by Hamlet, who criticizes Laertes's intense mourning. They struggle until they are parted by the mourners and Hamlet leaves annoyed, with Horatio in his wake. Claudius and Gertrude are now convinced of Hamlet's insanity and the king suggests to Laertes that they put their sinister plan into practice without delay.

Annotations:

2   *salvation:* i.e. damnation – the gravedigger confuses the two words

4   *straight:* immediately; properly (fitting a Christian burial)
      the crowner hath sat on her: the coroner (a public officer) has held an investigation

9   *se offendendo:* 'self-offence'; wrong for Latin *se defendendo* (self-defence)

10 *wittingly:* knowingly
      argues: proves

11 *branches:* sides to it

12 *argal:* wrong for Latin *ergo* (therefore)

13 *goodman:* title for a person below the rank of gentleman, followed by the occupation
      delver: gravedigger

16 *will he, nill he:* whether he wants to or not

21 *quest law:* law of inquests (official investigations into deaths)

25 *there thou say'st:* how right you are

26 *countenance:* permission

ACT V

Scene I

Elsinore. A churchyard.

Enter two CLOWNS *[*GRAVEDIGGERS *with spades and pickaxes].*

FIRST CLOWN: Is she to be buried in Christian burial, when she wilfully seeks her own salvation?

SECOND CLOWN: I tell thee she is, therefore make her grave straight. The crowner hath sat on her, and finds it Christian
5   burial.

FIRST CLOWN: How can that be, unless she drowned herself in her own defence?

SECOND CLOWN: Why, 'tis found so.

FIRST CLOWN: It must be *se offendendo*, it cannot be else. For here
10   lies the point: if I drown myself wittingly, it argues an act, and an act hath three branches – it is to act, to do, and to perform. Argal, she drowned herself wittingly.

SECOND CLOWN: Nay, but hear you, goodman delver –

FIRST CLOWN: Give me leave. Here lies the water – good. Here
15   stands the man – good. If the man go to this water and drown himself, it is will he, nill he, he goes – mark you that. But if the water come to him and drown him, he drowns not himself. Argal, he that is not guilty of his own death shortens not his own life.

20 **SECOND CLOWN:** But is this law?

FIRST CLOWN: Ay, marry, is't, crowner's quest law.

SECOND CLOWN: Will you ha' the truth on't? If this had not been a gentlewoman, she should have been buried out o' Christian burial.

25 **FIRST CLOWN:** Why, there thou sayst! And the more pity that great folk should have countenance in this world to drown or hang

27   *even-Christen:* fellow Christians
28   *ditchers:* those who dig channels or drains
29   *Adam's profession:* in the Bible, Adam had to look after the Garden of Eden
28   *bore arms:* had a coat of arms/had arms to dig with
33   *heathen:* non-believer
34   *scripture:* the Bible
36   *purpose:* point
     confess thyself: '... and be hanged' – proverb, i.e. 'confess and bear the consequences'
37   *go to:* get on with it
39   *mason:* bricklayer
     shipwright: shipbuilder
     carpenter: sb. who makes and repairs wooden structures
40   *gallows-maker:* sb. who makes wooden structures to hang criminals
     frame: structure
41   *tenants:* lodgers, residents
48   *unyoke:* stop working
51   *Mass:* by the holy (Catholic) Mass
52   *cudgel:* beat with a stick
53   *mend his pace:* go faster
56   *stoup:* cup

themselves more than their even-Christen. Come, my spade; there is no ancient gentlemen but gardeners, ditchers, and grave-makers. They hold up Adam's profession.

30 **SECOND CLOWN:** Was he a gentleman?

FIRST CLOWN: He was the first that ever bore arms.

SECOND CLOWN: Why, he had none.

FIRST CLOWN: What, art a heathen? How dost thou understand the scripture? The scripture says Adam digged. Could he
35 dig without arms? I'll put another question to thee. If thou answerest me not to the purpose, confess thyself –

SECOND CLOWN: Go to!

FIRST CLOWN: What is he that builds stronger than either the mason, the shipwright, or the carpenter?

40 **SECOND CLOWN:** The gallows-maker; for that frame outlives a thousand tenants.

FIRST CLOWN: I like thy wit well, in good faith. The gallows does well, but how does it well? It does well to those that do ill. Now, thou dost ill to say the gallows is built stronger than the church.
45 Argal, the gallows may do well to thee. To't again, come.

SECOND CLOWN: Who builds stronger than a mason, a shipwright, or a carpenter?

FIRST CLOWN: Ay, tell me that, and unyoke.

SECOND CLOWN: Marry, now I can tell!

50 **FIRST CLOWN:** To't.

SECOND CLOWN: Mass, I cannot tell.

Enter HAMLET *and* HORATIO *afar off.*

FIRST CLOWN: Cudgel thy brains no more about it, for your dull ass will not mend his pace with beating; and when you are asked this question next, say 'a grave-maker'. The houses he
55 makes last till doomsday. Go, get thee to Yaughan, fetch me a stoup of liquor.

Exit SECOND CLOWN.

59   *contract:* pass
        behove: amusement
60   *meet:* better
63   *custom … easiness:* habit has made him indifferent to his task
64–65   *the hand … sense:* is more sensitive
67   *clawed me in his clutch:* caught me in his grasping fist
68   *shipped me intil the land:* put me into the earth
69   *been such:* been young and in love
71   *knave:* rascal
        jowls: throws

Note, l. 71: The biblical Cain killed his brother Abel with a donkey's jawbone (*Kieferknochen*).

72   *pate:* head
73   *o'erreaches:* outwits, gains an advantage by being clever
        circumvent: outwit
81   *my Lady Worm's:* belonging to the worms, i.e. dead
        chopless: without jawbones
82   *mazard:* head
        sexton: gravedigger
83   *revolution:* change of fortune
84   *breeding:* raising
        loggets: Elizabethan game with sticks that are thrown at a stake in the
        ground

[Sings]
In youth when I did love, did love,
Methought it was very sweet
To contract-o the time for-a my behove,

60   *O, methought there-a was nothing-a meet.*

HAMLET: Has this fellow no feeling of his business, that he sings at grave-making?

HORATIO: Custom hath made it in him a property of easiness.

HAMLET: 'Tis e'en so. The hand of little employment hath the

65   daintier sense.

FIRST CLOWN: *[Sings]*
But age with his stealing steps
Hath clawed me in his clutch,
And hath shipped me intil the land,
As if I had never been such.

Throws up a skull.

70   **HAMLET:** That skull had a tongue in it, and could sing once. How the knave jowls it to th' ground, as if 'twere Cain's jawbone, that did the first murder! This might be the pate of a politician which this ass now o'erreaches, one that would circumvent God, might it not?

75   **HORATIO:** It might, my lord.

HAMLET: Or of a courtier, which could say 'Good morrow, sweet lord! How dost thou, good lord?' This might be my Lord Such-a-one, that praised my Lord Such-a-one's horse when he meant to beg it, might it not?

80   **HORATIO:** Ay, my lord.

HAMLET: Why, e'en so, and now my Lady Worm's, chopless, and knocked about the mazard with a sexton's spade. Here's fine revolution, and we had the trick to see't. Did these bones cost no more the breeding but to play at loggets with 'em? Mine ache

85   to think on't.

87 *for and:* and furthermore
shrowding sheet: cloth a dead body is wrapped in before burial
88 *clay: Lehm*
89 *meet:* fitting
91 *quiddities:* detailed differences of meaning, subtleties
quillets: cunning arguments
92 *tenures: Pachtverträge*
93 *sconce:* head
94 *battery:* physical attack
95 *statutes:* legal documents securing debts
recognizances: legal documents formally accepting a debt
96 *fines:* legal documents concerning land property
double vouchers: zwei Bürgen
recoveries: legal processes securing land ownership
96–97 *the fine of his fines:* the end of his lawsuits regarding land ownership
90 *pate:* head
91 *vouch:* guarantee
100 *pair of indentures:* joint agreement with each person keeping half of the
document
conveyances: legal document of ownership
101 *box:* 1. box for documents; 2. coffin
inheritor: person who receives property from a person who dies
103 *jot:* bit
104 *parchment:* material used for writing on
106–107 *they are … in that:* people who seek security in legal documents are
simpletons
107 *sirrah:* title to address persons of lower rank
115 *the quick:* the living

FIRST CLOWN: *[Sings]*
> *A pickaxe and a spade, a spade,*
> *For and a shrouding sheet,*
> *O, a pit of clay for to be made,*
> *For such a guest is meet.*

Throws up another skull.

90 **HAMLET:** There's another. Why may not that be the skull of a lawyer? Where be his quiddities now, his quillets, his cases, his tenures, and his tricks? Why does he suffer this rude knave now to knock him about the sconce with a dirty shovel, and will not tell him of his action of battery? Hum! This fellow might be in's

95 time a great buyer of land, with his statutes, his recognizances, his fines, his double vouchers, his recoveries. Is this the fine of his fines, and the recovery of his recoveries, to have his fine pate full of fine dirt? Will his vouchers vouch him no more of his purchases, and double ones too, than the length and breadth

100 of a pair of indentures? The very conveyances of his lands will scarcely lie in this box; and must th' inheritor himself have no more, ha?

HORATIO: Not a jot more, my lord.

HAMLET: Is not parchment made of sheepskins?

105 **HORATIO:** Ay, my lord, and of calves' skins too.

HAMLET: They are sheep and calves which seek out assurance in that. I will speak to this fellow. Whose grave's this, sirrah?

FIRST CLOWN: Mine, sir.
> *[Sings] O, a pit of clay for to be made*
110 > *For such a guest is meet.*

HAMLET: I think it be thine indeed, for thou liest in't.

FIRST CLOWN: You lie out on't, sir, and therefore 'tis not yours. For my part, I do not lie in't, yet it is mine.

HAMLET: Thou dost lie in't, to be in't and say it is thine. 'Tis for the
115 dead, not for the quick; therefore thou liest.

FIRST CLOWN: 'Tis a quick lie, sir, 'twill away again from me to you.

124 *absolute:* accurate; literal
     by the card: precisely
125 *equivocation:* double meaning, verbal ambiguity
126 *picked:* over-refined
128 *galls his kibe:* steps on his heels
145 *ground:* cause
150 *pocky corses:* people who died of syphilis
     hold the laying in: hold together long enough to be buried

HAMLET: What man dost thou dig it for?

FIRST CLOWN: For no man, sir.

HAMLET: What woman then?

120 **FIRST CLOWN:** For none neither.

HAMLET: Who is to be buried in't?

FIRST CLOWN: One that was a woman, sir, but, rest her soul, she's
dead.

HAMLET: How absolute the knave is! We must speak by the card,
125   or equivocation will undo us. By the Lord, Horatio, this three
years I have taken note of it: the age is grown so picked that the
toe of the peasant comes so near the heel of the courtier, he
galls his kibe. How long hast thou been a grave-maker?

FIRST CLOWN: Of all the days i' th' year, I came to't that day that
130   our last King Hamlet o'ercame Fortinbras.

HAMLET: How long is that since?

FIRST CLOWN: Cannot you tell that? Every fool can tell that. It was
the very day that young Hamlet was born, he that is mad and
sent into England.

135 **HAMLET:** Ay, marry, why was he sent into England?

FIRST CLOWN: Why, because he was mad. He shall recover his wits
there; or, if he do not, 'tis no great matter there.

HAMLET: Why?

FIRST CLOWN: 'Twill not be seen in him there. There the men are
140   as mad as he.

HAMLET: How came he mad?

FIRST CLOWN: Very strangely, they say.

HAMLET: How, strangely?

FIRST CLOWN: Faith, e'en with losing his wits.

145 **HAMLET:** Upon what ground?

FIRST CLOWN: Why, here in Denmark. I have been sexton here,
man and boy, thirty years.

HAMLET: How long will a man lie i' th' earth ere he rot?

FIRST CLOWN: Faith, if he be not rotten before he die, as we have
150   many pocky corses nowadays that will scarce hold the laying in,

151 *tanner:* workman producing leather from animal skin

154 *his hide is so tanned:* his skin is so dry

155–156 *sore decayer:* violent destroyer

156 *whoreson:* (intensifier) wretched

157 *lien you:* lain

162 *pestilence:* plague

163 *flagon:* bottle

164 *jester:* clown employed by kings

168 *fancy:* imagination

170 *abhorred:* filled with horror
     my gorge rises: I feel like throwing up

172 *gibes:* jokes
     gambols: high leaps

173 *were wont ... roar:* used to make everyone laugh roaringly at dinner

174 *chop-fallen:* miserable

176 *favour:* facial appearance

179 *Alexander:* Alexander the Great (356–323 BC), king of Macedonia and ruler
     of the Persian empire

he will last you some eight year or nine year. A tanner will last you nine year.

HAMLET: Why he more than another?

FIRST CLOWN: Why, sir, his hide is so tanned with his trade that
155   he will keep out water a great while, and your water is a sore decayer of your whoreson dead body. Here's a skull now: this skull hath lien you i' th' earth three and twenty years.

HAMLET: Whose was it?

FIRST CLOWN: A whoreson mad fellow's it was. Whose do you
160   think it was?

HAMLET: Nay I know not.

FIRST CLOWN: A pestilence on him for a mad rogue! He poured a flagon of Rhenish on my head once. This same skull, sir, was Yorick's skull, the king's jester.

165 **HAMLET:** This?

FIRST CLOWN: E'en that.

HAMLET: Let me see. *[Takes the skull.]* Alas, poor Yorick! I knew him, Horatio, a fellow of infinite jest, of most excellent fancy, he hath borne me on his back a thousand times – and now how
170   abhorred in my imagination it is! My gorge rises at it. Here hung those lips that I have kissed I know not how oft. Where be your gibes now? Your gambols? Your songs? Your flashes of merriment that were wont to set the table on a roar? Not one now, to mock your own grinning? Quite chop-fallen? Now get you to
175   my lady's chamber, and tell her, let her paint an inch thick, to this favour she must come. Make her laugh at that. – Prithee, Horatio, tell me one thing.

HORATIO: What's that, my lord?

HAMLET: Dost thou think Alexander looked o' this fashion
180   i' th' earth?

HORATIO: E'en so.

HAMLET: And smelt so? Pah!

Puts down the skull.

186 *stopping a bunghole:* closing the hole in a barrel
187 *too curiously:* too complicated
188–189 *with modesty enough:* without exaggeration
191 *loam: Tonerde*
196 *t'expel the winter's flaw:* to keep out the winter wind
199 *maimèd rites:* ceremony not having everything it should have
    betoken: mean
200 *desperate:* suicidal
201 *fordo:* take
    estate: high rank
202 *couch:* hide
    mark: observe
206 *obsequies:* funeral ceremony
207 *warranty:* official permission
    doubtful: suspicious
208 *and but … order:* the king's command has overruled the God-given order
209 *unsanctified:* not made holy

HORATIO: E'en so, my lord.

HAMLET: To what base uses we may return, Horatio! Why may
185   not imagination trace the noble dust of Alexander, till he find it
stopping a bunghole?

HORATIO: 'Twere to consider too curiously to consider so.

HAMLET: No, faith, not a jot, but to follow him thither with
modesty enough, and likelihood to lead it, as thus: Alexander
190   died, Alexander was buried, Alexander returneth to dust, the
dust is earth, of earth we make loam, and why of that loam
whereto he was converted might they not stop a beer barrel?
Imperious Caesar, dead and turned to clay,
Might stop a hole to keep the wind away.
195   *O, that that earth which kept the world in awe*
Should patch a wall t'expel the winter's flaw!
But soft, but soft! Aside! Here comes the king,
The queen, the courtiers.

Enter PRIESTS *with a coffin in funeral procession,* KING, QUEEN,
LAERTES, *with* LORDS *attendant.*

                                        Who is this they follow?
And with such maimèd rites? This doth betoken
200   The corse they follow did with desperate hand
Fordo its own life. 'Twas of some estate.
Couch we awhile, and mark.

Retires with HORATIO.

LAERTES: What ceremony else?

HAMLET: That is Laertes, a very noble youth. Mark.
205 **LAERTES:** What ceremony else?

PRIEST: Her obsequies have been as far enlarged
As we have warranty. Her death was doubtful,
And but that great command o'ersways the order,
She should in ground unsanctified have lodged

210 *the last trumpet:* doomsday
        for: instead of
211 *shards:* broken pieces of pottery
        flints: hard stones used to start a fire
        pebbles: small, round stones
212 *crants:* garlands
213 *strewments:* flowers scattered on the grave
213–214 *the bringing home of bell:* burying her with a funeral bell ringing
216 *profane* (v): disrespect
217 *sage requiem:* solemn hymn for the dead
        such rest: the same rest
218 *peace-parted:* departed in peace
220 *churlish:* insensitive, rude
221 *ministering:* doing service for God
222 *liest howling:* suffer in hell
225 *decked:* decorated with flowers
226 *treble:* three times
228 *ingenious sense:* intelligent mind
229 *deprived:* robbed
233 *o'ertop:* be higher than
        Pelion: mountain in Greece
234 *Olympus:* mountain in Greece, home of the ancient Greek gods

210 Till the last trumpet. For charitable prayers,
Shards, flints, and pebbles should be thrown on her.
Yet here she is allowed her virgin crants,
Her maiden strewments, and the bringing home
Of bell and burial.

215 **LAERTES:** Must there no more be done?

PRIEST: No more be done.
We should profane the service of the dead
To sing sage requiem and such rest to her
As to peace-parted souls.

LAERTES: Lay her i' th' earth;
And from her fair and unpolluted flesh

220 May violets spring. I tell thee, churlish priest,
A ministering angel shall my sister be
When thou liest howling.

HAMLET: What, the fair Ophelia?

GERTRUDE: Sweets to the sweet! Farewell.

Scatters flowers.

I hoped thou shouldst have been my Hamlet's wife;

225 I thought thy bride-bed to have decked, sweet maid,
And not t 'have strewed thy grave.

LAERTES: O, treble woe
Fall ten times treble on that cursèd head
Whose wicked deed thy most ingenious sense
Deprived thee of. Hold off the earth awhile,

230 Till I have caught her once more in mine arms.

Leaps in the grave.

Now pile your dust upon the quick and dead
Till of this flat a mountain you have made
T' o'ertop old Pelion or the skyish head
Of blue Olympus.

237 *conjures the wandering stars:* has magical power over the planets

238 *wonder-wounded:* struck with surprise

   • *grapples:* struggles

242 *splenitive:* passionate

245 *pluck them asunder:* pull them apart

246 *quiet:* calm

248 *wag:* open and shut

252 *make up my sum:* match mine

254 *forbear him:* leave him alone

255 *thou't:* you will

256 *woo't:* would you

257 *eisel:* vinegar

235 **HAMLET:** *[Comes forward]* What is he whose grief
       Bears such an emphasis? Whose phrase of sorrow
       Conjures the wandering stars, and makes them stand
       Like wonder-wounded hearers? This is I,
       Hamlet the Dane.

Leaps in after LAERTES.

   LAERTES: The devil take thy soul!

Grapples with him.

240 **HAMLET:** Thou pray'st not well.
       I prithee take thy fingers from my throat,
       For though I am not splenitive and rash,
       Yet have I in me something dangerous
       Which let thy wisdom fear. Hold off thy hand.
245 **CLAUDIUS:** Pluck them asunder.
   GERTRUDE: Hamlet, Hamlet!
   ALL: Gentlemen!
   HORATIO: Good my lord, be quiet.

The ATTENDANTS *part them, and they come out of the grave.*

   HAMLET: Why, I will fight with him upon this theme
       Until my eyelids will no longer wag.
   GERTRUDE: O my son, what theme?
250 **HAMLET:** I loved Ophelia. Forty thousand brothers
       Could not with all their quantity of love
       Make up my sum. What wilt thou do for her?
   CLAUDIUS: O, he is mad, Laertes.
   GERTRUDE: For love of God, forbear him!
255 **HAMLET:** 'Swounds, show me what thou't do.
       Woo't weep, woo't fight, woo't fast, woo't tear thyself?
       Woo't drink up eisel, eat a crocodile?

259 *outface:* outdo

261 *prate:* speak in an angry way

262–263 *our ground ... zone:* the earth burns its head against the sun

264 *Ossa:* mountain in Greece

    and thou'lt mouth: if you're going to speak in a loud and angry way

265 *rant:* speak in a loud and angry way

268 *golden couplets are disclosed:* baby birds with yellow feathers have hatched

269 *his silence will sit drooping:* he will become quiet

273 *dog have his day:* a dog cannot always be stopped from acting like a dog

274 *wait upon him:* watch him closely

275–276 *in our last night's speech:* by remembering my speech of last night

277 *the present push:* immediate action

279 *living:* lasting

I'll do't. Dost thou come here to whine,
To outface me with leaping in her grave?
260 Be buried quick with her, and so will I.
And if thou prate of mountains, let them throw
Millions of acres on us, till our ground,
Singeing his pate against the burning zone,
Make Ossa like a wart! Nay, and thou'lt mouth,
265 I'll rant as well as thou.

GERTRUDE: This is mere madness;
And thus a while the fit will work on him.
Anon, as patient as the female dove
When that her golden couplets are disclosed,
His silence will sit drooping.

HAMLET: Hear you, sir!
270 What is the reason that you use me thus?
I loved you ever – but it is no matter.
Let Hercules himself do what he may,
The cat will mew, and dog will have his day.

Exit.

CLAUDIUS: I pray thee, good Horatio, wait upon him.

Exit HORATIO.

275 *[To* LAERTES*]* Strengthen your patience in our last night's
speech.
We'll put the matter to the present push.
Good Gertrude, set some watch over your son.
This grave shall have a living monument.
280 An hour of quiet shortly shall we see,
Till then in patience our proceeding be.

Exeunt.

Summary:

In the hall of Elsinore Castle, Hamlet tells Horatio how he substituted an order for his execution with a new one, so that Rosencrantz and Guildenstern will be killed when the ship reaches England. Hamlet feels no twinge of guilt about their fate. When Osric, a courtier, comes to tell the prince that Claudius proposes a fencing duel between Hamlet and Laertes, he readily accepts. The king wagers that Hamlet will score three more hits than Laertes in a dozen rounds of fencing. When Horatio cautions Hamlet against the fight with Laertes, Hamlet tells his friend that he is ready to die and fears nothing. The court enters and Hamlet asks Laertes's pardon, assuring him that his deeds were done in moments of madness, which is not entirely accepted by Laertes. They fight and Hamlet scores two hits. Meanwhile, Claudius has prepared the poisoned wine and urges Hamlet to take it as refreshment in a pause, which the prince postpones. Gertrude toasts her son and unknowingly drinks the poison before Claudius can stop her. Laertes succeeds in wounding Hamlet with the poisoned sword tip. In the ensuing scuffle and now earnest fight, the swords are exchanged and Hamlet wounds Laertes fatally. Gertrude exclaims that the drink was poisoned and dies. Laertes reveals the murder plot and casts all blame on Claudius. Furious, Hamlet stabs his uncle and forces the poisoned wine down his throat. Laertes absolves Hamlet of his own and Polonius's death before he dies, while Hamlet forgives Laertes for killing him. Hamlet insists that Horatio tells his story and clears his name. Horatio mourns Hamlet, who dies in peace. Fortinbras, who has returned from Poland, enters together with the ambassadors from England, who report that Rosencrantz and Guildenstern were executed as Claudius requested. Horatio promises to tell what led to the bloody scene. Fortinbras takes command, claims the Danish throne and pays a tribute to Hamlet as the bodies are carried out.

Annotations:

6 *mutines in the bilboes:* rebels in chains
8 *indiscretion:* instinct, intuition
9 *pall:* become uninteresting
    learn: teach
10 *ends:* destiny, death
11 *rough-hew:* roughly plan
13 *sea-gown:* clothes worn on a ship
    scarfed: wrapped loosely
15 *fingered their packet:* searched and stole their bundle of letters
    in fine: finally
19 *knavery:* villainy
20 *larded:* embellished
21 *importing:* concerning
22 *bugs and goblins in my life:* terrors to be feared if I continued living
23 *supervise* (n): first reading
    leisure bated: time wasted
24 *stay:* await

Scene II

Elsinore. A hall in the castle.

Enter HAMLET *and* HORATIO.

HAMLET: So much for this, sir, now shall you see the other.
    You do remember all the circumstance?
HORATIO: Remember it, my lord!
HAMLET: Sir, in my heart there was a kind of fighting
5   That would not let me sleep. Methought I lay
    Worse than the mutines in the bilboes. Rashly,
    And praised be rashness for it – let us know,
    Our indiscretion sometime serves us well
    When our deep plots do pall, and that should learn us
10   There's a divinity that shapes our ends,
    Rough-hew them how we will –
HORATIO: That is most certain.
HAMLET: Up from my cabin,
    My sea-gown scarfed about me, in the dark
    Groped I to find out them, had my desire,
15   Fingered their packet, and in fine withdrew
    To mine own room again, making so bold
    My fears forgetting manners, to unseal
    Their grand commission; where I found, Horatio –
    O royal knavery! – an exact command,
20   Larded with many several sorts of reasons,
    Importing Denmark's health, and England's too,
    With, ho, such bugs and goblins in my life,
    That, on the supervise, no leisure bated,
    No, not to stay the grinding of the axe,
25   My head should be struck off.
HORATIO: Is't possible?
HAMLET: Here's the commission, read it at more leisure.
    But wilt thou bear me how I did proceed?

29 *benetted round:* surrounded
30 *or ... brains:* before I could stop myself
32 *fair:* in neat handwriting
33 *statists:* statesmen
34 *baseness:* that which is fitting for a low rank
36 *yeoman:* independent farmer, known to be loyal
37 *effect:* nature
38 *conjuration:* solemn appeal, entreaty
39 *tributary:* country owing payment after a lost war
40 *palm:* palm-tree, a symbol of peace
41 *wheaten garland:* garland made of wheat straws symbolising prosperity
42 *stand a comma ... amities:* i.e. there was only a short break in the friendship between England and Denmark
43 *'as'es:* sentences beginning with 'as', a pun on 'asses'
      charge: importance
45 *debatement:* consideration
47 *shriving time:* time to confess their sins
48 *ordinant:* directing, in control
49 *signet:* ring used as a seal
51 *writ:* letter
52 *subscribed:* signed
      gave't th'impression: sealed it
53 *changeling:* replacement
54 *was sequent:* followed
59 *insinuation:* intervention, scheming
60 *baser nature:* those of lower social status

HORATIO: I beseech you.

HAMLET: Being thus benetted round with villainies,
30 Or I could make a prologue to my brains,
They had begun the play. I sat me down,
Devised a new commission, wrote it fair.
I once did hold it, as our statists do,
A baseness to write fair, and laboured much
35 How to forget that learning; but, sir, now
It did me yeoman's service. Wilt thou know
Th' effect of what I wrote?

HORATIO: Ay, good my lord.

HAMLET: An earnest conjuration from the king,
As England was his faithful tributary,
40 As love between them like the palm might flourish,
As peace should still her wheaten garland wear
And stand a comma 'tween their amities,
And many suchlike 'as'es of great charge,
That, on the view and knowing of these contents,
45 Without debatement further, more, or less,
He should the bearers put to sudden death,
Not shriving time allowed.

HORATIO: How was this sealed?

HAMLET: Why, even in that was heaven ordinant.
I had my father's signet in my purse,
50 Which was the model of that Danish seal;
Folded the writ up in the form of th' other,
Subscribed it, gave 't th' impression, placed it safely,
The changeling never known. Now, the next day
Was our sea-fight, and what to this was sequent
55 Thou know'st already.

HORATIO: So Guildenstern and Rosencrantz go to 't.

HAMLET: Why, man, they did make love to this employment.
They are not near my conscience. Their defeat
Does by their own insinuation grow.
60 'Tis dangerous when the baser nature comes

61   *pass* (n): thrust with a sword
       fell incensèd points: fierce, deadly sword points
63   *does ... upon:* don't you think that it is my duty
65   *popped ... hopes:* pushed himself in before I could become king
66   *thrown ... life:* is plotting my death
67   *cozenage:* treachery, deceit
68   *quit:* repay
69   *canker of our nature:* spreading disease of humanity
69–70   *come in further evil:* become more evil
72   *issue:* outcome
73   *interim:* period of time between two events
74   *to say 'one':* a short moment
77–78   *by the image ... of his:* we are similar in our concerns, i.e. we both want revenge
78   *court his favours:* be friendly towards him
79   *bravery:* extravagance
80   *towering passion:* intense fury
83   *waterfly:* i.e. a buzzing insect
85   *gracious:* fortunate
87   *crib:* place
       mess: banquet table
       chough: kind of bird (*Dohle*); chatterer
88   *spacious in the possession of dirt:* possesses large areas of land
89   *impart:* tell

Between the pass and fell incensèd points
Of mighty opposites.

HORATIO: Why, what a king is this!

HAMLET: Does it not, think thee, stand me now upon –
He that hath killed my king, and whored my mother,

65   Popped in between th' election and my hopes,
Thrown out his angle for my proper life,
And with such cozenage – is 't not perfect conscience
To quit him with this arm? And is 't not to be damned
To let this canker of our nature come

70   In further evil?

HORATIO: It must be shortly known to him from England
What is the issue of the business there.

HAMLET: It will be short. The interim is mine,
And a man's life's no more than to say 'one'.

75   But I am very sorry, good Horatio,
That to Laertes I forgot myself,
For by the image of my cause, I see
The portraiture of his. I'll court his favours.
But sure the bravery of his grief did put me

80   Into a towering passion.

HORATIO: Peace! Who comes here?

Enter young OSRIC, *a courtier.*

OSRIC: Your lordship is right welcome back to Denmark.

HAMLET: I humbly thank you, sir. *[Aside to* HORATIO*]* Dost know
this waterfly?

HORATIO: *[Aside to* HAMLET*]* No, my good lord.

85   **HAMLET:** *[Aside to* HORATIO*]* Thy state is the more gracious; for 'tis
a vice to know him. He hath much land, and fertile; let a beast
be lord of beasts, and his crib shall stand at the king's mess. 'Tis
a chough, but, as I say, spacious in the possession of dirt.

OSRIC: Sweet lord, if your lordship were at leisure, I should impart

90   a thing to you from his Majesty.

91 *diligence:* due attention
bonnet: cap or hat usually worn indoors
95 *indifferent:* moderately
96 *sultry:* oppressively hot
97 *complexion:* temperament; constitution
99 *signify:* announce
104 *excellent differences:* extraordinary accomplishments
soft society: pleasing manners
105 *great showing:* excellent appearance
105–106 *the card or calender:* an excellent model
106 *gentry:* nobility, gentlemanly behaviour
106–107 *the continent … see:* every quality a gentleman requires
108 *definement:* definition, description
perdition: loss
109 *divide him inventorially:* list his qualities
dozy th' arithmetic of memory: confuse you completely
110 *yaw:* zig-zag
his quick sail: its straight course
111 *in the verity of extolment:* to praise him truthfully
of great article: highly accomplished
112 *infusion:* qualities, talents
110 *dearth:* uniqueness
112–113 *make true diction:* speak truly
113 *semblable:* likeness
114 *trace:* draw
umbrage: shadow
115 *infallibly:* absolutely truthful
116 *concernancy:* relevance, purpose
117 *more rawer breath:* cruder words
119 *in another tongue:* i.e. in less pompous language
119–120 *you will to't:* you should try harder
121 *what … gentleman:* why are you speaking of this gentleman?

HAMLET: I will receive it, sir, with all diligence of spirit. Put your
bonnet to his right use. 'Tis for the head.

OSRIC: I thank your lordship, it is very hot.

HAMLET: No, believe me, 'tis very cold; the wind is northerly.

95 **OSRIC:** It is indifferent cold, my lord, indeed.

HAMLET: But yet methinks it is very sultry and hot for my
complexion.

OSRIC: Exceedingly, my lord, it is very sultry, as 'twere – I cannot
tell how. But, my lord, his Majesty bade me signify to you that

100   he has laid a great wager on your head. Sir, this is the matter –

HAMLET: I beseech you remember.

HAMLET *moves him to put on his hat.*

OSRIC: Nay, good my lord, for mine ease, in good faith. Sir, here is
newly come to court Laertes; believe me, an absolute gentleman, full of most excellent differences, of very soft society and

105   great showing. Indeed, to speak feelingly of him, he is the card
or calendar of gentry, for you shall find in him the continent of
what part a gentleman would see.

HAMLET: Sir, his definement suffers no perdition in you, though I
know to divide him inventorially would dozy th' arithmetic of

110   memory, and yet but yaw neither in respect of his quick sail. But
in the verity of extolment, I take him to be a soul of great article,
and his infusion of such dearth and rareness as, to make true
diction of him, his semblable is his mirror, and who else would
trace him, his umbrage, nothing more.

115 **OSRIC:** Your lordship speaks most infallibly of him.

HAMLET: The concernancy, sir? Why do we wrap the gentleman in
our more rawer breath?

OSRIC: Sir?

HORATIO: Is 't not possible to understand in another tongue? You

120   will to 't, sir, really.

HAMLET: What imports the nomination of this gentleman?

OSRIC: Of Laertes?

129 *lest:* unless
131 *imputation:* reputation
132 *meed:* merit; worth
     unfellowed: unparalleled
134 *rapier:* light sword
     dagger: short weapon-like knife (*Dolch*)
136 *Barbary:* Arab
137 *impawned:* wagered, bet
138 *poniards:* daggers
     assigns: accessories
     girdle: belt
     hangers: straps on sword belts holding the swords
139 *carriages:* hangers
     dear to fancy: tasteful
140 *responsive to the hilts:* fitting the sword handles
140–141 *of very liberal conceit:* with highly imaginative decorations
143 *edified by the margent:* in need of an explanation
146 *germane:* suitable, relevant
152 *laid:* bet
     passes: rounds
153 *not exceed you three hits:* must score three more hits than Hamlet to win
154 *trial:* contest
155 *vouchsafe the answer:* accept the challenge
157 *the opposition of your person:* presenting yourself as opponent

HORATIO: His purse is empty already. All's golden words are spent.

HAMLET: Of him, sir.

125 **OSRIC:** I know you are not ignorant –

HAMLET: I would you did, sir, yet, in faith, if you did, it would not much approve me. Well, sir?

OSRIC: You are not ignorant of what excellence Laertes is.

HAMLET: I dare not confess that, lest I should compare with him in

130 excellence, but to know a man well were to know himself.

OSRIC: I mean, sir, for his weapon; but in the imputation laid on him by them, in his meed he's unfellowed.

HAMLET: What's his weapon?

OSRIC: Rapier and dagger.

135 **HAMLET:** That's two of his weapons, but well.

OSRIC: The king, sir, hath wagered with him six Barbary horses, against the which he has impawned, as I take it, six French rapiers and poniards, with their assigns, as girdle, hangers, and so. Three of the carriages, in faith, are very dear to fancy, very

140 responsive to the hilts, most delicate carriages, and of very liberal conceit.

HAMLET: What call you the carriages?

HORATIO: I knew you must be edified by the margent ere you had done.

145 **OSRIC:** The carriages, sir, are the hangers.

HAMLET: The phrase would be more germane to the matter if we could carry cannon by our sides; I would it might be hangers till then. But on, six Barbary horses against six French swords, their assigns, and three liberal-conceited carriages – that's the

150 French bet against the Danish. Why is this all impawned, as you call it?

OSRIC: The king, sir, hath laid, sir, that in a dozen passes between yourself and him, he shall not exceed you three hits; he hath laid on twelve for nine, and it would come to immediate trial if

155 your lordship would vouchsafe the answer.

HAMLET: How if I answer no?

OSRIC: I mean, my lord, the opposition of your person in trial.

159 *the breathing time:* time for exercise
    foils: weapons used for fencing
160 *and the king hold his purpose:* and if the king keeps his promise
163 *redeliver you:* report back what you said
164 *after what flourish:* however extravagantly you want to express it
165 *commend my duty:* dedicate my service
167–168 *no tongues else for's turn:* no one will praise Osric
169 *lapwing:* type of bird (*Kiebitz*)
169 *with the shell on his head:* immediately after hatching
170 *he did comply … dug:* he paid formal compliments to his nurse's breast
171 *bevy:* flock, group
    drossy: frivolous, worthless
172 *dotes on:* is fond of
    got the tune of the time: uses fashionable speech
172–173 *outward habit of encounter:* custom of social interaction
173 *yesty collection:* fashionable words and manners
174 *fanned and winnowed:* wise and considered
175 *blow them to their trial:* test their opinions
    the bubbles are out: they don't know what to say
176 *commended him:* sent his compliments
172 *attend:* wait for
178 *if your pleasure hold:* if you are still ready
    play: fence
180 *am constant to my purposes:* keep my promise
181 *his fitness speaks:* he is ready to fight
184 *in happy time:* at the right time
185 *gentle entertainment:* courteous welcome
186 *fall:* begin

HAMLET: Sir, I will walk here in the hall. If it please his Majesty, it
is the breathing time of day with me. Let the foils be brought,
160 the gentleman willing, and the king hold his purpose, I will win
for him if I can. If not, I will gain nothing but my shame and the
odd hits.

OSRIC: Shall I redeliver you e'en so?

HAMLET: To this effect, sir, after what flourish your nature will.

165 **OSRIC:** I commend my duty to your lordship.

HAMLET: Yours, yours.

Exit OSRIC.

He does well to commend it himself, there are no tongues else
for's turn.

HORATIO: This lapwing runs away with the shell on his head.

170 **HAMLET:** He did comply with his dug before he sucked it. Thus
has he, and many more of the same bevy that I know the drossy
age dotes on, only got the tune of the time and outward habit
of encounter, a kind of yesty collection, which carries them
through and through the most fanned and winnowed opinions;
175 and do but blow them to their trial, the bubbles are out.

Enter a LORD.

LORD: My lord, his Majesty commended him to you by young
Osric, who brings back to him that you attend him in the hall.
He sends to know if your pleasure hold to play with Laertes, or
that you will take longer time.

180 **HAMLET:** I am constant to my purposes; they follow the king's
pleasure. If his fitness speaks, mine is ready; now or whenso-
ever, provided I be so able as now.

LORD: The king and queen and all are coming down.

HAMLET: In happy time.

185 **LORD:** The queen desires you to use some gentle entertainment to
Laertes before you fall to play.

190 *at the odds:* according to the bets (cf. V, ii, 152–153)
193 *gaingiving:* misgiving, doubt
195–196 *forestall their repair hither:* prevent their coming here
197 *not a whit:* not at all
    defy augury: reject predictions
    providence: foresight; divine intention
198 *sparrow:* type of bird (*Spatz, Sperling*)
200 *no man ... leaves:* no one knows the meaning of life
201 *betimes:* early
205 *this presence:* everyone here
206 *sore distraction:* painful mental derangement
208 *exception:* bitterness, wish for revenge

HAMLET: She well instructs me.

Exit LORD.

HORATIO: You will lose this wager, my lord.

HAMLET: I do not think so. Since he went into France, I have been
190   in continual practice. I shall win at the odds. But thou wouldst
not think how ill all's here about my heart – but it is no matter.

HORATIO: Nay, good my lord.

HAMLET: It is but foolery, but it is such a kind of gaingiving as
would perhaps trouble a woman.

195 **HORATIO:** If your mind dislike anything, obey it. I will forestall
their repair hither and say you are not fit.

HAMLET: Not a whit, we defy augury. There is special providence in
the fall of a sparrow. If it be now, 'tis not to come; if it be not to
come, it will be now; if it be not now, yet it will come. The readi-
200   ness is all. Since no man knows of aught he leaves, what is 't to
leave betimes? Let be.

Enter KING, QUEEN, LAERTES, OSRIC *and* LORDS, *with other*
ATTENDANTS *with foils and daggers.*

CLAUDIUS: Come, Hamlet, come, and take this hand from me.

HAMLET *takes* LAERTES *by the hand.*

HAMLET: Give me your pardon, sir, I've done you wrong;
But pardon 't, as you are a gentleman.
205   This presence knows, and you must needs have heard,
How I am punished with sore distraction.
What I have done,
That might your nature, honour, and exception
Roughly awake, I here proclaim was madness.
210   Was 't Hamlet wronged Laertes? Never Hamlet.
If Hamlet from himself be ta'en away,

215 *faction:* party
218 *disclaiming:* denying
     purposed: intentional
220–221   *have shot ... brother:* have hurt you by accident
221 *in nature:* as a son, i.e. as far as his private feelings are concerned
223 *in terms of honour:* i.e. as far as my honour as a public person is concerned
219 *stand aloof:* will be distant/not involved
225 *some elder ... honour:* qualified experts
221 *voice and precedent of peace:* support for reconciliation
227 *my name ungored:* my reputation uninjured
230 *frankly:* freely
232 *foil:* i.e. background against which a jewel shows extra sparkle
234 *stick fiery off:* stand out and sparkle brilliantly
238 *laid the odds:* made a bet
240 *bettered:* thought to be better
     odds: advantage; i.e. Laertes has to score three hits more than Hamlet

And when he's not himself does wrong Laertes,
Then Hamlet does it not, Hamlet denies it.
Who does it, then? His madness. If 't be so,
215 Hamlet is of the faction that is wronged,
His madness is poor Hamlet's enemy.
Sir, in this audience,
Let my disclaiming from a purposed evil
Free me so far in your most generous thoughts,
220 That I have shot my arrow o'er the house
And hurt my brother.

LAERTES: I am satisfied in nature,
Whose motive in this case should stir me most
To my revenge. But in my terms of honour
I stand aloof, and will no reconcilement
225 Till by some elder masters of known honour
I have a voice and precedent of peace
To keep my name ungored. But till that time
I do receive your offered love like love,
And will not wrong it.

HAMLET: I embrace it freely,
230 And will this brother's wager frankly play.
Give us the foils. Come on.

LAERTES: Come, one for me.

HAMLET: I'll be your foil, Laertes. In mine ignorance
Your skill shall, like a star i' th' darkest night,
Stick fiery off indeed.

LAERTES: You mock me, sir.

235 **HAMLET:** No, by this hand.

CLAUDIUS: Give them the foils, young Osric. Cousin Hamlet,
You know the wager?

HAMLET: Very well, my lord.
Your Grace has laid the odds o' th' weaker side.

CLAUDIUS: I do not fear it, I have seen you both,
240 But since he is bettered, we have therefore odds.

LAERTES: This is too heavy, let me see another.

242 *likes me:* pleases me
have all a length: are all of the same length
244 *stoup: Trinkbecher*
246 *quit:* wins
247 *ordnance:* cannons
248 *better breath:* increased energy
249 *union:* pearl
252 *kettle:* kettledrum, *Kesselpauke*
256 *wary:* watchful
262 *palpable:* obvious; definite

HAMLET: This likes me well. These foils have all a length?

OSRIC: Ay, my good lord.

Prepare to play.

CLAUDIUS: Set me the stoups of wine upon that table.
245   If Hamlet give the first or second hit,
       Or quit in answer of the third exchange,
       Let all the battlements their ordnance fire.
       The king shall drink to Hamlet's better breath,
       And in the cup an union shall he throw
250   Richer than that which four successive kings
       In Denmark's crown have worn. Give me the cups,
       And let the kettle to the trumpet speak,
       The trumpet to the cannoneer without,
       The cannons to the heavens, the heaven to earth,
255   'Now the king drinks to Hamlet!' Come, begin.
       And you the judges, bear a wary eye.

HAMLET: Come on, sir.

LAERTES: Come, my lord.

They play.

HAMLET: One.
260 **LAERTES:** No.

HAMLET: Judgement!

OSRIC: A hit, a very palpable hit.

LAERTES: Well, again!

CLAUDIUS: Stay, give me drink. Hamlet, this pearl is thine.
265   Here's to thy health.

Drum; trumpets sound; a shot goes off.

Give him the cup.

266 *bout:* round
269 *fat:* unfit; sweaty
     scant of: short of
270 *napkin:* handkerchief
271 *carouses:* drinks; toasts
280 *dally:* delay
281 *pass:* attack with force
282 *make a wanton of me:* toy with me

HAMLET: I'll play this bout first; set it by awhile.
Come.

They play.

Another hit. What say you?
LAERTES: A touch, a touch, I do confess 't.
CLAUDIUS: Our son shall win.
GERTRUDE: He's fat, and scant of breath.
270   Here, Hamlet, take my napkin, rub thy brows.
The queen carouses to thy fortune, Hamlet.
HAMLET: Good madam!
CLAUDIUS: Gertrude, do not drink.
GERTRUDE: I will, my lord, I pray you pardon me.

Drinks.

275   **CLAUDIUS:** *[Aside]* It is the poisoned cup. It is too late.
HAMLET: I dare not drink yet, madam, by and by.
GERTRUDE: Come, let me wipe thy face.
LAERTES: My lord, I'll hit him now.
CLAUDIUS: I do not think 't.
LAERTES: *[Aside]* And yet it is almost against my conscience.
280   **HAMLET:** Come for the third, Laertes. You do but dally.
Pray you pass with your best violence.
I am afeard you make a wanton of me.
LAERTES: Say you so? Come on.

Play.

OSRIC: Nothing neither way.
285   **LAERTES:** Have at you now!

LAERTES *wounds* HAMLET, *in scuffling, they change rapiers.*

286 *incensed:* out of control
291 *as a woodcock … springe:* i.e. caught in my own trap like a foolish bird
293 *sounds:* faints
302 *unbated and envenomed:* sharp and poisonous

CLAUDIUS: Part them! They are incensed.

HAMLET: Nay, come again.

He wounds LAERTES. *The* QUEEN *falls.*

OSRIC: Look to the queen there, ho!

HORATIO: They bleed on both sides. How is it, my lord?

290 **OSRIC:** How is 't, Laertes?

LAERTES: Why, as a woodcock to mine own springe, Osric.
    I am justly killed with mine own treachery.

HAMLET: How does the queen?

CLAUDIUS: She sounds to see them bleed.

GERTRUDE: No, no, the drink, the drink! O my dear Hamlet!

295   The drink, the drink! I am poisoned.

Dies.

HAMLET: O villainy! Ho, let the door be locked.
    Treachery! Seek it out!

LAERTES *falls.*

LAERTES: It is here, Hamlet. Hamlet, thou art slain,
    No medicine in the world can do thee good,

300   In thee there is not half an hour of life.
    The treacherous instrument is in thy hand,
    Unbated and envenomed. The foul practice
    Hath turned itself on me. Lo, here I lie,
    Never to rise again. Thy mother's poisoned.

305   I can no more. The king – the king's to blame.

HAMLET: The point envenomed too! Then, venom, to thy work.

Hurts the KING.

ALL: Treason! Treason!

310   *potion:* poisonous drink
311   *is justly served:* got what he deserved
312   *tempered:* mixed
318   *chance:* bad luck
319   *mutes:* silent watchers
320   *fell:* cruel
324   *the unsatisfied:* the uninformed
325   *antique Roman:* i.e. ancient Roman who prefers suicide to an unworthy life
327   *I'll ha't:* I'll have it
328   *wounded name:* tarnished reputation
331   *absent* [- ʹ-] *thee from felicity:* leave happiness behind

CLAUDIUS: O, yet defend me, friends! I am but hurt.

HAMLET: Here, thou incestuous, murderous, damnèd Dane,

310   Drink off this potion! Is thy union here?
    Follow my mother.

KING *dies.*

LAERTES: He is justly served.
    It is a poison tempered by himself.
    Exchange forgiveness with me, noble Hamlet.
    Mine and my father's death come not upon thee,
315   Nor thine on me.

Dies.

HAMLET: Heaven make thee free of it! I follow thee.
    I am dead, Horatio. Wretched queen, adieu!
    You that look pale and tremble at this chance,
    That are but mutes or audience to this act,
320   Had I but time, as this fell sergeant, death,
    Is strict in his arrest – O, I could tell you –
    But let it be. Horatio, I am dead,
    Thou liv'st; report me and my cause aright
    To the unsatisfied.

HORATIO: Never believe it.

325   I am more an antique Roman than a Dane.
    Here's yet some liquor left.

HAMLET: As th' art a man,
    Give me the cup. Let go! By heaven, I'll ha 't.
    O good Horatio, what a wounded name
    Things standing thus unknown, shall live behind me!

330   If thou didst ever hold me in thy heart,
    Absent thee from felicity awhile,
    And in this harsh world draw thy breath in pain,
    To tell my story.

334 *conquest: victory*

336 *warlike volley:* gunfire salute

337 *o'ercrows:* triumphs over

339–340 *prophesy ... Fortinbras:* foresee he will be elected King of Denmark

341–342 *with th' occurrents ... solicited:* together with everything that has
           happened so that ... (Hamlet leaves the sentence unfinished)

347 *aught:* anything
         cease: stop

348 *quarry:* heap of dead bodies
         cries on havoc: suggests slaughter

349 *toward:* being prepared

350 *at a shot:* at one stroke

351 *dismal:* depressing

353 *senseless:* without sense or feeling

March afar off, and shot within.

What warlike noise is this?

OSRIC: Young Fortinbras, with conquest come from Poland,

335   To the ambassadors of England gives

This warlike volley.

HAMLET: O, I die, Horatio!

The potent poison quite o'ercrows my spirit.

I cannot live to hear the news from England,

But I do prophesy th'election lights

340   On Fortinbras; he has my dying voice.

So tell him, with th'occurrents, more and less,

Which have solicited – the rest is silence.

Dies.

HORATIO: Now cracks a noble heart. Good night, sweet prince,

And flights of angels sing thee to thy rest. –

345   Why does the drum come hither?

Enter FORTINBRAS *and* ENGLISH AMBASSADORS, *with drum, col-
ours and* ATTENDANTS.

FORTINBRAS: Where is this sight?

HORATIO: What is it you will see?

If aught of woe or wonder, cease your search.

FORTINBRAS: This quarry cries on havoc. O proud death,

What feast is toward in thine eternal cell

350   That thou so many princes at a shot

So bloodily hast struck.

AMBASSADOR: The sight is dismal,

And our affairs from England come too late.

The ears are senseless that should give us hearing,

To tell him his commandment is fulfilled

359 *so jump upon:* precisely
    question: affair
365 *carnal:* connected with the body or with sex
361 *judgements:* punishments
    casual: happening by chance
367 *put on:* brought about
    by cunning and forced cause: on false and fabricated grounds
368 *upshot:* outcome, conclusion
373 *rights of memory:* unforgotten rights; i.e. the reasons why he prepared for
    war with Denmark (I, 1)
374 *vantage:* good fortune
376 *draw on:* encourage
378 *wild:* disturbed
381 *put on:* made king
382 *passage:* funeral march
383 *rites:* rituals

355 That Rosencrantz and Guildenstern are dead.
Where should we have our thanks?
HORATIO: Not from his mouth,
Had it th' ability of life to thank you.
He never gave commandment for their death.
But since, so jump upon this bloody question,
360 You from the Polack wars, and you from England,
Are here arrived, give order that these bodies
High on a stage be placèd to the view,
And let me speak to th' yet unknowing world
How these things came about. So shall you hear
365 Of carnal, bloody and unnatural acts,
Of accidental judgements, casual slaughters,
Of deaths put on by cunning and forced cause;
And, in this upshot, purposes mistook
Fallen on th' inventors' heads. All this can I
370 Truly deliver.
FORTINBRAS: Let us haste to hear it,
And call the noblest to the audience.
For me, with sorrow I embrace my fortune.
I have some rights of memory in this kingdom,
Which now to claim my vantage doth invite me.
375 **HORATIO:** Of that I shall have also cause to speak,
And from his mouth whose voice will draw on more.
But let this same be presently performed,
Even while men's minds are wild, lest more mischance
On plots and errors happen.
FORTINBRAS: Let four captains
380 Bear Hamlet like a soldier to the stage,
For he was likely, had he been put on,
To have proved most royal; and for his passage,
The soldiers' music and the rites of war
Speak loudly for him.
385 Take up the bodies. Such a sight as this

386 *shows much amiss:* is very improper

- *peal of ordnance:* gun salute

Becomes the field, but here shows much amiss.
Go, bid the soldiers shoot.

Exeunt marching, after which a peal of ordnance is shot off.

William Shakespeare

Considering that he is probably the most famous playwright who ever lived, surprisingly little is known about William Shakespeare, Britain's national poet and Man of the Millennium. He was born in Stratford-upon-Avon in April 1564 and educated in the local grammar school. His father was a glove maker and a member of the town council. At 18, he married Anne Hathaway, with whom he had three children, Susanna and twins Hamnet and Judith. Other than that, little else is known about Shakespeare until the year 1592, when he

William Shakespeare (Chandos portrait, between 1600 and 1610)

is mentioned as being a playwright in London. It is also known that he worked as an actor and that he was part owner of a company of actors called 'The Lord Chamberlain's Men'. They soon became the leading London theatre company and enjoyed Queen Elizabeth's patronage. In 1599, they built their own theatre on the south bank of the River Thames, called the *Globe*. After the queen's death in 1603, King James also awarded them a royal patent and the troupe was renamed 'The King's Men'. Shakespeare became a wealthy man and bought properties in London and Stratford. He retired to Stratford in around 1614 and died there on 23 April 1616. Few records of Shakespeare's life survive, and there has been considerable speculation about such matters as his physical appearance, sexuality, religious beliefs, and whether the works attributed to him were in fact written truly by him.

During his lifetime Shakespeare wrote 38 plays. He may have written more but if he did, the manuscripts have not survived. Although 18 of his plays were published during his lifetime, most of these editions (called 'quartos') were probably not overseen by Shakespeare. Their texts may have been reconstructed from memory by members of the cast of the plays. It was only in 1623 that his plays were first published by two of his former colleagues in what is called the 'First Folio'. Since Shakespeare was dead by the time the First Folio was published, it cannot be said that it is a definitive text. That does not change the fact, however, that this was the first time that many of Shakespeare's plays were printed together.

Shakespeare is unusual in that he wrote a wide variety of plays. Not only did he write history plays that covered over a hundred years of English history when the two Houses of Plantagenet fought for the crown, he was also equally competent at tragedy (e.g. *Macbeth*) as well as comedy (e.g. *Much Ado about Nothing*). Shakespeare was very good at turning older plays or stories from Greek or Roman mythology into new plays. Besides being a playwright, he was also a prolific poet: he wrote a cycle of 154 sonnets as well as several long poems.

Shakespeare's reputation grew slowly after his death, but by the end of the 20th century he had become the most performed dramatist in the world. Some theatre companies have been devoting their repertoire almost exclusively to the performance of his plays, like Shakespeare's Globe in London or the Royal Shakespeare Company (RSC) in Stratford-upon-Avon. There are annual international festivals in his name, and British institutions like the BBC and the British Council produce media to help people understand his language and to facilitate an approach to his dramas. Many of the lines from his plays and poems are still well known today. Since his death, his works have remained relevant and have inspired adaptations and spin-offs in different art forms throughout the centuries. Since he never judges human behaviour and experience, Shakespeare's characters and their relationships and conflicts have remained timeless and are shown in a touching way that audiences or readers can still relate to. He has also coined an astonishing number of new words and managed to evoke gripping moods, all the while giving his characters definitive voices. His complex or heightened language makes use of many rhetorical figures that make his lines so memorable. It is thought that he has contributed thousands of words to the English language. Shakespeare's inventiveness and creativity laid the groundwork that helped English become the universal language that it is today.

Shakespeare's Theatre

The first commercial theatre in England was simply called 'The Theatre' and was built in 1576 by James Burbage, who would later become Shakespeare's associate. The London Common Council forbade theatres within the city walls and people commonly regarded actors and playwrights as low-life citizens, only slightly better than criminals. Next to the theatre buildings outside the city, one could find other entertainments like taverns, brothels, cockfighting or bear-baiting arenas. Even though it was forbidden, Burbage built his theatre on the shore of the Thames River, in Shoreditch. Shakespeare and his actors then managed to secure the patronage of a nobleman and later even that of the monarch, which resulted in the acceptance of the theatre's location. They became popular entertainment at Queen Elizabeth's and King James's court. Their financial success gave Shakespeare and his shareholders the funds to build the Globe playhouse, shaped liked a wooden 'O', in 1599. There, James Burbage's son Richard, Will Kempe, Edward Alleyn and other actors performed in the plays Shakespeare wrote for many years and established their excellent reputation.

Inside the rebuilt Globe Theatre

Shakespeare may have found his love for the theatre by watching trave-ling acting companies who came to the countryside where he was living in his youth. The troupes would transport their property on wagons and use inns or courtyards to perform their plays because no buildings for theatres existed. They mostly showed religious stories or scenes taken from the Bible, which meant to teach viewers moral lessons. During the Renaissance, the plays would become less religious and would be based on Greek or Roman legends, or have historical events as their plot.

The Master of the Revels, a public official, had to read and approve every play to be performed and could shut down a theatre completely. During times of plague or social or political riots, authorities would close the theatres, which they feared were places of moral corruption. Audi-ences were packed with people from all walks of life – it is said that a full house at the Globe numbered about 3000 spectators. The rich patrons sat on the stage or on gallery seats, whereas the poorer visitors, called 'groundlings', stood in front of the stage which was about a metre above the ground. These 'groundlings' paid a penny for the entertainment, which was a day's wages. Audience behaviour was quite different then, with people eating, drinking and smoking during the performance, and even heckling actors or throwing things at them. Shakespeare wrote for his diverse audience and adapted his language, the characters, actions and situations so as to appeal to all social levels of his society.

The theatre buildings were round and roofless with a thrust stage (pro-jecting out into the audience) and plays were staged during the day. A performance could take half a day – today Shakespeare's plays are usually cut because they can last up to four hours, like *Hamlet*. The bare stage had little scenery, and props would be carried on by the players in full view of the audience, because there were no breaks or intervals. If a scene was set at night, the actors would comment on the moon or stars in the sky to indicate the hour of the day. The actors did not wear cos-tumes indicating the time in which the plays were set, but their normal clothes. However, they often wore elegant hand-me-down clothes from the upper classes on stage.

Most plays were rehearsed for just a day or two, they ran only for a short time and actors had to learn their parts for a new play quickly.

Full scripts did not exist and the actors had paper slips that only had their own lines with the cues of the previous speaker so that they knew when to speak. Some theatres staged up to four different plays within a week. Because women were not permitted to act on stage until 1660, female roles were performed by boys and young men. As Shakespeare often used the motif of cross-dressing, when female characters (played by boys) dressed as boys on stage, it allowed much room for double meaning.

The Globe burned down in 1613 after the roof caught fire when a cannon was fired during a performance.

In 1642, the Puritans, a very strict religious faction that saw performing and watching plays as immoral, succeeded in lobbying for the closing of the theatres altogether. Theatres did not reopen until Charles II came to the throne 18 years later. By then, many of the theatrical traditions of Shakespeare's theatre were lost, and the new theatres of the Restoration period viewed and staged his plays very differently.

In the 1990s, a reconstruction of the old Globe was built very close to its original site, where visitors today can experience plays the way Elizabethans did.